Happy Years…and Many More

Dr. Edward F. Coffman, Jr.

Happy Years...and Many More

An Autobiography
Edward F. Coffman, Jr.

St. Louis, Missouri

Copyright © 2012 by Edward F. Coffman, Jr.

All rights reserved. No part of this book may be reproduced or transmitted in any form or by any means, electronic or mechanical, including photocopying, recording, or by any information storage and retrieval system, without permission in writing from the copyright owner. For permission to reuse content, please contact Connie Hitchcock, hitchcockconnie@gmail.com

Print ISBN: 9781603500326

Published by Lucas Park books   www.lucasparkbooks.com

Printed in United States of America

THE AUTHOR

Edward F. Coffman, Jr., born in Russellville, Kentucky, January 25, 1922, the son of Emma Hill and Edward F. Coffman. Graduated from Russellville High School, 1938. Vanderbilt University, A.B., 1942, B.D., 1944, D.Min., 1972. Northeast Missouri State Teachers College (now Truman University), M.A. in Guidance, 1967. Ordained to Ministry at First Christian Church, Russellville, Ky., 1944. Director of Youth Work and Choir, Eastside Christian Church, Nashville, Tn. Student pastorates at Daysville (Logan County), Bethlehem (Hopkins County), and Sinking Fork (Christian County) in Kentucky. Pastor First Christian Church, Leitchfield, Ky., Director of Religious Education, First Christian Church, Mayfield, Ky., Associate and Campus Minister, First Christian Church, Columbia, Mo. Pastor First Church, Kirksville, Mo., and First Christian Church, Madisonville, Ky. Interim Ministries at Christian Churches in Middlesboro, Ky., Huntsville, Al., Greenville, Ky., Bowling Green, Ky., Paducah, Ky., Chattanooga, Tn., and Guthrie, Ky.

OTHER PUBLICATIONS

Logan County, Kentucky, A Pictorial History (Narration), 1988
First Christian Church, Russellville, Kentucky 1941-1991, 1991
Through My Father's Eyes—The Story of Logan County, Kentucky, 2004

THESIS

Thomas Miller Allen—Pioneer Evangelist, 1972

My Life Log

January 25, 1922	Born, Russellville, Kentucky
November 1927	Baptized, First Christian Church
1934 – 1938	Russellville High School
June 1942	AB, Vanderbilt University, Nashville, Tn.
January 1943	Director of Youth Work and Choir, East Side Christian Church, Nashville, Tn.
1943 – 1945	Student Pastor of Christian Churches at Daysville, (Logan County), Bethlehem, (Hopkins County), and Sinking Fork (Christian County), Kentucky
November 9, 1944	Ordained, First Christian Church, Russellville
March 1945	Enlisted in Marine Corps for Chaplaincy School but was never called up.
June 1945	BD, Vanderbilt Divinity School
1945 – 1946	Pastor, First Christian Church, Leitchfield, Ky.
1946	Director of Religious Education, First Christian Church, Mayfield, Ky.
1946 – 1958	Associate Pastor and Campus Minister, First Christian Church, Columbia, Mo.
June 5, 1949	Married Carol Jean Alexander, Columbia, Mo.
1958 – 1967	Pastor, First Christian Church, Kirksville, Mo.
1967 – 1987	Pastor, First Christian Church, Madisonville, Ky.
1972 – 1987	Director of Development, Christian Church Homes of Ky.
June 1968	MA in Guidance, Northeast Missouri State Teachers College, Kirksville, Mo. (now Truman University)
June 1972	D.Min., Vanderbilt University Divinity School
March 1974	Emmaus Walk
1979 – 1980	President, Christian Church in Kentucky
June 30, 1987	Retired
1988 – 1997	Interim Ministries at Middlesboro, Ky., Huntsville, Al., Greenville, Ky., Bowling Green, Ky., Paducah, Ky., Chattanooga, Tn., and Guthrie, Ky.
2003 – 2004	Lt. Governor, Kiwanis, Kentucky-Tennessee District

To
Carol Jean
For
Sixty Years of Devotion

Following is a brief remembrance of Carol's life as excerpted from a presentation at her funeral, written by our daughter Connie:

The treasured daughter of the late Frank and Lenora Alexander, Carol Jean Alexander was born in Boone County Missouri on November 13, 1926 and passed from this life on August 23, 2009 at her home in Russellville, Kentucky.

The Alexander family moved from the country into Columbia, Missouri when Carol was three years old. Throughout her childhood, she was surrounded by a wealth of cousins and dear friends. She was a beautiful young ballerina. As a graduate of Hickman High School, she was always proud to be a "Hickman High Kewpie". Carol attended Christian College in Columbia and attained her A.A. degree. She then transferred to the University of Missouri where she earned her B.S. in Home Economics.

From her father, she learned the value of living life to the fullest and finding enjoyment in even simple things. From her mother, she learned to be a gracious and welcoming hostess, making all who came in to her presence feel at home. These ideals shaped our mother into a woman of great talent for creating warmth and smiles wherever she went.

The Alexanders were active in the First Christian Church in Columbia, and one day a young minister arrived that soon became Carol's one and only true love, a love that lasted more than 60 years. After a one year courtship, Edward F. Coffman and Carol Jean Alexander were married on June 5, 1949 in front of 900 of their closest friends at the church in Columbia. From that point forward she became the devoted wife of a minister and a vital partner in her husband's ministry.

In 1958, Carol and Ed moved to Kirksville, Missouri. Shortly thereafter, Carol began to teach part-time at a local pre-school. That part-time job soon turned into a passion built upon Carol's love of children. Following their move to Madisonville, Kentucky in 1967, Carol founded the First Christian Church Pre-School where she impacted a bevy of 3 and 4 year olds until her retirement 20 years later. Many of these former pre-schoolers remained in touch with her through the years.

When Ed "retired" from full-time ministry in 1987, so did Carol and she was duly recognized at that time for her long and devoted service both to the congregation they served and the Pre-School she founded. Never one to be idle long, they embarked upon a series of nine Interim ministries that took them all over Kentucky and into Tennessee and Alabama.

Throughout her life, Carol was an avid reader, volunteer, and world traveler. She was involved in the Prosody Club, Aftermath, Habitat for Humanity, Historic Russellville, Christian Women's Fellowship, and P.E.O. Dedicated to life long learning, P.E.O., a women's organization devoted to enabling women to pursue educational opportunities, was the perfect outlet for Carol's interests. She actively participated in her local chapters, organized several chapters from Missouri to Kentucky, and served as a state officer and President of the Kentucky Chapter.

While her leaving saddens us all, her spirit will fill our hearts forever.

CONTENTS

1	Early Life and Family	1
2	Vanderbilt Years	19
3	Seminary Years and the Beginning of Ministry	27
4	Columbia, Missouri	36
5	Kirksville, Missouri	52
6	Madisonville, Kentucky	66
7	The Interim Years	88
Epitaph		107

Acknowledgments

I deeply appreciate my daughters – Catherine Paluch, Carol Coffman, and Constance Hitchcock – for their encouraging me to write the story of my life, for their information, memories and pictures. I owe Connie a debt of gratitude for her help in getting the book published. We worked through the Christian Board of Publication with the good help of Gail Stobaugh, Lynne Condellone, and Lucas Park Books. Thank you all.

Preface

by Constance Hitchcock

My father is a remarkable man. Born in 1922, he is from a generation that grew up on simple things...swimming in a rock quarry, spending time with friends playing games and dancing, going on picnics with the family, learning at the knees of aunts, uncles and grandparents, working in creative occupations to make enough spending money for a movie. He has lived through major changes in our lives...from World War II to the terrorist attacks of 9/11, from dependence on radio and newspapers for most communication to the era of 24 hour information sources such as television, computers, and cell phones, from the times when hard times were truly hard and not made by our own desires for more and more. He watched the landing of the first man on the moon, saw the entire era of the space shuttle program, and is now witnessing the pictures being sent back from Mars. He spent his entire education and ministry typing on typewriters, and today has mastered the use of a computer (well almost!). He has traveled the United States many times over, and seen much of the world. He has suffered great loss. And all the while, he has remained thankful for the simple pleasures in life and true to what I see as his core values....that God is a loving God who will care for us always, that we are created to enjoy God's creation and preserve it and progress it for the good of one another and to God's glory, and that we are to use God's gifts to us in service to others.

Following in his father's footsteps for most of his life, my dad still left his own unique stamp. He was a true minister...serving the needs of his congregations in the most personal ways. While always a good speaker, his gift was in his ability to be there for people, to share even the darkest of their moments with comfort and love. We received calls at all hours at our house, from those in the congregation certainly, but also from all sorts of folks in our communities, from even some just passing through town. He never turned down a request for a help. He was a servant leader in all his endeavors, leading by example, motivating others by showing he would do the hard work too, and encouraging others to reach for their dreams. He built churches, literally and figuratively, by understanding the needs of the congregations. He has touched, and continues to touch, so many lives through his generous and giving spirit.

My husband always enjoys hearing my dad's "stories". Dad's recollections are always entertaining and engaging. We have spent many hours sitting around the dinner table listening. I am glad he decided to write down many of his memories. It is not all here, couldn't be, but what you will find are the highlights of his life. Note that most always the memories are about not his successes, but about the people in his life and how they influenced him. I hope he realizes how much he has influenced all of us.

In writing this autobiography, he has articulated his memories. In sharing this autobiography, he leaves a legacy of a life well lived. We can learn much from my father who has persevered through hardships, made the most of joyous opportunities, and remained devoted throughout to his God, his family and especially the love of his life, my mother.

Happy Years...and Many More

In 1964 my father, Edward Coffman, published his autobiography which he called *Happy Years*. Now I wish to do the same, using his title Happy Years, but adding a phrase ...*And Many More.* This comes from Carol's mother, Lenora Alexander, who always added those words after every wish for birthdays or anniversaries.

1

Early Life and Family

My life began in the Hill family home at 680 East Second Street, Russellville, Kentucky. Born January 25, 1922, I was the second child of Edward and Emma Hill Coffman, born as was the custom in those days at home. That home was the long-time residence of the family of Robert Zachary and Mary Evelina Bowling Clark Hill. Mother had been reared there by her uncle Tom and her aunts Lou and Lizzie. They were like my grandparents, for mother's mother had died soon after she was born and her father Robert Tucker Hill asked his siblings to care for her, which they did in a beautiful way. She grew up in a warm and loving atmosphere, which I came to appreciate as I also was the recipient of their love as a child. From them I received a rich background of old-time wisdom and appreciation for family life and nature. It was Uncle Tom who taught me to understand much of early farm life. It was Aunt Lizzie who imbued me with a love of nature and wildlife.

The Hill family had come from Virginia to Logan County in 1835 and lived for a time on a farm near Auburn before buying the home at 680 East Second Street (then Barclay Street). My great-uncle, Thomas Maddux Hill, had built and operated an ice factory in Auburn for many years. He lived there in the summer season in a room at the rear of the plant. I spent a few days with him occasionally as a small child. It was in the front office of the plant that I learned to play chess at night. He took his meals at the Blewett home a few blocks away. In the winter he lived in the family home in Russellville and ran a coal yard. His horse and wagon and later a small model-T truck stayed in the two story barn at the back of our lot. My great-aunts, Mary Lewis Hill and Harriet Elizabeth Hill, were like my grandparents when I was growing up. Aunt Lou was the early housekeeper who died in 1928. Aunt Lizzie had been a very fine artist who taught art at one time at Logan College. We have many of her paintings still in our home in Russellville, the big one of an old castle is over the mantel in our living room. She was also a musician, playing a ladies size guitar which had been brought over the mountains by Aunt Missouri from Virginia. It is still a fine instrument that was to go to the next in the family who learned to play it. Connie Sue decided that she should have it so she took guitar lessons from her aunt Polly Coffman and played it through school and still uses it today. While playing for a CYF Conference at Camp Kum-Ba-Ya she learned that it was actually a very valuable Martin guitar, valued at several thousand dollars. I was very close to uncle Tom and aunt Lizzie. Her death in 1936 was hard for me, as was uncle Tom's in 1939 when I was a freshman at Vanderbilt.

Much of my early life was spent in the Hill family home with the tutelage of my aunts and uncle. My sister Emma Hill and my brother Bradley were all born there and we grew up during the depression years. One of my earliest memories was of walking to the end of the block and meeting Paul Summers. I told him I was three years old, and learned that he was a year older. We became friends and remained so throughout our lives, graduating from school together. I started to school at the age of six. I was very small growing up. I had pneumonia three times in my early years, once so severe that the doctors left saying there was nothing more to do but pray. But their prayers were answered.

I started school in the first grade with Miss Fannie Bryan. She taught me to read real well at an early time. Dorothy Ann Evans was in my class and one day her father, Byrne Evans, stopped me on the street and asked me how well I was reading. I replied that I read about like Dorothy Ann did. "How well is that?" he asked. Just about perfect, I told him, and he repeated that all over town. I wasn't too modest, but from that day I have enjoyed reading and still make it a major part of my life.

Our home on Second Street was quite rural, reflecting the farm life from which the Hill family had come. Back of our yard was a rose garden with many different flowers. I remember especially a large bed of canna lilies. On the other side was a hen house and large area for chickens. Beyond it was a two story barn where Uncle Tom kept his horse and later his model T Ford which he used in his work. Still farther back was a large plot that for years was a vegetable garden which Uncle Tom and then Dad kept full. Later we made that lot into a tennis court which we used until we moved up to Grandmother Coffman's home on Seventh Street.

There was an open field across the street from our house on Second Street where all the neighborhood kids played ball of every kind. I was so poor at most games that when we chose up sides for teams, I was always the last one to be included. But I learned to do something quite well. There was a long limb on a tree in our backyard which I used for a trapeze. I spent long hours on that trapeze, becoming quite adept at swinging high to jump from it, or hanging by my knees or heels. There was no one else in the neighborhood who was as good as I was on that trapeze. This helped to make up for my lack of prowess in softball or football. I suppose you would call this compensation. In later years, I have used the trapeze as a symbol of my effort to succeed. I also learned that I could climb trees quite well. Because I was small I could climb higher than many others. One day I climbed to the top of a tree at the back of Granville Clark's home and pulled myself up one more limb.. But coming down, I missed the limb and fell clear through the tree with my back to the trunk, finally straddling the last limb before hitting the ground. I was terribly skinned and sore and coming home spent the rest of the day in bed.

One day when I was probably five years old I was allowed to walk to town by myself, about a mile. I met Dad at his Rotary Club luncheon and sometime later wrote that they sang "Here comes old Hezzie, he is always late." I didn't really understand this until much later when my own Kiwanis club sometimes sang the same about me. After lunch Dad and I went over to the park where there was a patriotic gathering of some kind. All the school children marched downtown to take part in the festivities. I spotted my sister in the group. I later wrote, "I said hi'dy to Sister and she said hi'dy to me." The gathering was in the city park in front of the monument to a Confederate soldier.

About that same time the two families that had bought lots from Grandmother Coffman were building their new homes. Again I was allowed to walk to town alone to visit Grandmother. The Beauchamps were building their brick house next door and I climbed on the basement walls. In the process I scuffed up my new pair of shoes that Mother had allowed me to wear on condition that I take good care of them. They were new because I had ruined my old shoes. I had walked in them in a puddle in front of the house and when I came in Mother set them on the open oven door of the kitchen stove to dry out. This was in the old days when our stove was kindled with coal and would stay warm for several hours after being used. Not realizing what it would do, I found the shoes and put them inside the oven while it was still very hot, which baked my shoes badly. So the new shoes that I wore that day were the ones which had been bought by my stupidity. Incidentally, Ed and Ann Proctor were building the brick house next door to the Beauchamps that same summer. Fortunately, I did not climb on their basement wall. Both of these two houses were built in 1927, filling in the two lots between our house and the cottage Grandmother had built some years before on the corner of Seventh and Winter Streets. These two families became great neighbors for years to come.

Around the corner from our home on Second Street was an old cemetery, long abandoned. Bradley and I and our friends often played in the cemetery round the broken monuments. Many years later I learned that John Littlejohn was buried there. He was a famous Methodist minister who had been a sheriff in Virginia. During the War of 1812 when Washington was being threatened by the British before they invaded the Capitol, President James Madison asked John Littlejohn to take the National Archives, including the Declaration of Independence and the Constitution for safe keeping, which he did until after the War. On October 4, 2008 I attended the dedication of a state Historical Marker for John Littlejohn in that cemetery where I had played as a boy.

My father was the Postmaster in Russellville, but after ten years, he decided he wanted to become a minister, which would make a decided change in our lives. When Dad left the Post Office and started studying for the ministry at the Vanderbilt University Divinity School, he and Mother were away a good deal. He spent the first year of his studies in Wesley Hall of the Divinity School, returning home each Saturday to preach for the First Christian Church which he was now serving as pastor. The second and third years he and Mother drove to Nashville three days a week. During this time Uncle Tom and Aunt Lizzie kept the home going and became even more like our grandparents. Before that we had a young woman who was studying at Bethel College after it had become co-educational.

She helped take care of us before her classes. I remember one time when she was giving Bradley a bath, which he resisted. He said, "Louise.Camera, why don't you go back to the farm."

Dad finished his work at Vanderbilt with two degrees and graduated with honors, receiving the Founder's Medal for the highest grades in the Divinity School. Mother, with no college experience after finishing two years of high school work, took a full load of both undergraduate and seminary courses, and received high praise from her professors. Bradley and I occasionally went with them to Vanderbilt on Saturdays. It was there that we met Dr. Tillett one day on the stairs of old Wesley Hall. He was Dad's theology professor and he told us to ask Dad why God made the devil. I remember hearing my first radio in the room of one of Dad's classmates, Ed Small.

I often visited my Grandmother Coffman as I was growing up and would go to see her after school, which was just two blocks from the Coffman home on Seventh Street. She loved to play rummy and playing with her I heard much of her travels. Julia Evans Coffman was the daughter of Selby Kennesaw and Rebecca Teeter Paris Evans. She was four years old when her father bought the home at 106 West Seventh Street (then Cedar Street) in 1866. Grandmother was my only living grandparent, and it was from her I learned of that side of my family. She and my grandfather Jacob Bradley Coffman were married August 7, 1889 in the Evans home and lived there until he died in 1912. Grandmother had graduated from Logan College in 1881 and taught school briefly in Brooksville, Florida where her sister Mrs. Clara E. Bailey lived. Through her sister she had numerous relatives in Florida, where she often visited in later years for several months at a time. After my grandfather died, she continued to live in her family home until her death at the age of ninety-five. The home on Seventh Street originally extended from 106 westward to Winter Street. I remember it having a barn at the rear and the foundations of several small houses along the alley. It had been built by Richard Curd, a banker, in 1814. The Curds lived in it until 1838 and it was sold several times until 1866. The original home was of two-story brick, but through the years it was enlarged several times until it is now like a freight train, extending back from the original building six rooms. After Dad and Mother were married they soon moved to the Hill home on Second Street. Grandmother then rented out the front part of the house. For many years Dorothy Wallace's parents, the Winston Stattons, lived there. Dorothy grew up in the home and was married in the living room. After my grandfather died, Grandmother built a cottage at the corner of the lot on Seventh and Winter Streets for investment purposes. It was rented through the years until after Dad died. In 1927 Grandmother sold two lots from the original home place to Dad's cousin Ed Proctor and his wife Anne, and to Emerson and Elizabeth (Bobs) Beauchamp, both of whom built very substantial homes that year as I noted earlier. Grandmother sold another corner on Winter Street to Miss Jane Perry.

Early Life and Family

In 1927 Dad agreed to become the pastor of his home church and fulfilled its duties quite well while going to school. The Christian Church at Berea, south of Russellville was without a pastor and for a year or more Dad served as its pastor once a month. We often were invited to dinner in the homes of church members. In this way I became friends with Charles Mac Noe and Martha Elizabeth Russell, who were my age. In l933 the depression made itself felt and the Russellville church reduced his work to half time. The same thing had happened with the First Christian Church of Greenville, so they worked out an arrangement for Dad to preach every other Sunday at each church. He would spend weekends in Greenville, staying at a small hotel downtown. I often went with him and acquired several new friends like John Shutt and Dorothy and Margaret McPherson. Greenville had a fine swimming pool which I thoroughly enjoyed.

It was during this time that my sister, Emma Hill, became ill. She had been the picture of health. She was a good student and was preparing to enter Vanderbilt, hopefully to study medicine. In the summer of 1933 she had attended summer conference at the conference grounds in Kuttawa, Kentucky when she became ill. The doctors were baffled and treated her as if she had diphtheria, but she was getting steadily weaker. Finally, Mother and Dad asked Dr. Gaithel Simpson, who was in Dad's Greenville church to come see her. The minute he walked in the room, Dr. Simpson said, "She has leukemia. You must get her to Nashville immediately." When they arrived at St. Thomas Hospital the doctors confirmed his diagnosis and told Mother and Dad that she could probably live only a few days. At that time, little was known of leukemia, either its cause or any effective treatment. They gave her cod liver oil, known only for anemia, and ordered blood transfusions. Sister had eleven transfusions in the next ten weeks. Mother and Dad gave nine of them and a man rooming where they were staying gave the other two. Transfusions at that time were arm to arm with the recipient. They enabled her to live nine weeks longer than had been predicted. Mother and Dad stayed with her constantly, Dad leaving only to preach on Sundays at his churches. They tried to keep our family going during that time they were living in Nashville. Aunt Lizzie and Uncle Tom kept our home well. Before leaving for Nashville Dad had secured Margie Pillow to stay in Russellville with them, She fixed breakfast each morning and began to prepare lunch before leaving. She stayed with us long after Sister died and was part of our family until she later moved to Nashville with some of her family.

Bradley and I went by bus to Nashville several weekends. Dad met us each time to take us to be with Sister. And he did his best to keep us in good spirits, taking us one time to see the Barnum and Bailey Ringling Brothers Circus. Many of Sister's friends came to see her during those long weeks. It was a most difficult time for us all and a somber night when they called to say that Sister had passed away and they were coming home. All our family members were waiting for them in the family home on Second Street. Someone asked how Emma would take this, and her sister Evelyn replied, "Emma will take this in the best possible way." Dad said, "It was indeed our Gethsemane. Our lovely daughter had left us and we had gone with her as far as it was possible to go. She quietly passed away and out of our sight. With faith in our hearts we hoped to see her another brighter, fairer day." Visitation was at our home on Second Street and the memorial service in the First Christian Church with two of Dad's pastoral colleagues officiating. Emma Hill was laid to rest in our new family lot in Maple Grove Cemetery, where Mother and Dad kept vigil at the cemetery each evening for many years. This was the first of two extremely difficult times for my parents. They also had to bid farewell to my brother Bradley in 1950 when he died of nephritis.

After my sister's death, Mother and Dad spent much time with her friends. They continued to come to our home and Mother and Dad often took them to the rock crusher pond on the Hopkinsville Road for swimming and picnics. It was there that I learned to swim in water that sloped down the old track to twenty feet or more. Those friends of my sister were very nice to me and for some time gave me lots of encouragement. One of these was Katherine Blakey, a school teacher who often asked me to grade her papers. Others were Mary McCarley, Teddy Townsend and Bess Matherly (later Mrs. Martin) who was a good friend of Mother and after we retired was a strong supporter of everything we did. Another was Otis Cooper, who had been reared by Dr. And Mrs. Landrum and who later said that he probably would have married my sister if she had lived.

Growing up in Russellville was most pleasant. Like everyone else, we had little money but we found simple pleasures to occupy our time. I remember my first job, not very pleasantly. I asked the manager of the Kroger store for a job after school. He told me to come to work on a Saturday and gave me sacks of apples to sell for ten cents each out on the sidewalk I saw people I knew who bought them readily. But I discovered that each bag had one bad piece of fruit below the top. When I complained to the manager that I thought this was not right, I soon lost my job. The next job I remember was at Andrews Drug Store. Bee Andrews or one of his brothers called me in and handed me a number of coupons good for free chocolate sodas. I was asked to give them to those I knew and in turn I could come in regularly for free sodas of my own. I don't know how many of those coupons I gave away, but I had my fill of chocolate sodas.

Bradley and I had one dog when we were growing up. Half-Pint must have been a stray that came to our house, but he soon was dearly loved by the family. He was a small ragamuffin who enjoyed the outdoors as well as life inside. We had him several years until one day we saw him cross the field in front of our house, but he never came home. We drove all over town looking for him, but finally decided that some disaster had befallen him. Not long after that I began to have difficulty with asthma, which we thought was due partly to dog dander, so we did not have another dog for many years. But we did have many cats through the years. Two of the best loved were my cat Margaret and Brad's Hoover.

I had many friends who lasted a lifetime. Talbott Mansfield lived around the corner on Fourth Street and we spent much time in each other's homes and

Early Life and Family

up the hillside to the edge of the knobs that surrounded Russellville. Talbott's mother Mildred was like another mother, and his sister, Maxine, like a sister. Talbott's father, Alderson Mansfield, ran the press at the local newspaper, the News Democrat.

I remember our neighbors on Second Street in Russellville. Next door to the east were the McClean family. This was the old family home of her mother's family, the Mortons. It was a beautiful old house on the corner of Second Street and Caldwell. One member of that family, Mr. Morton, wrote hymns, one of which is in our hymnal. There was a well kept yard between our house and theirs. I remember a large fish pond with special large species. Our cat found those fish attractive and often cleaned out the pond. Mr. Oss McClean was a jeweler who played the Aeolian harp beautifully. He played for the wedding of Mother and Dad in 1916. I remember a lovely wedding early one morning in their side yard when Dad had the ceremony and Mr. Oss played his harp. Many years later after he died, his daughter Clara Louise, then, Mrs. Henry Jones, gave the harp to Historic Russellville for the Bibb House where it is displayed with his music. In the yard at the edge of our two houses was a green apple tree. It was attractive to our neighbors, so Bradley and I would sell buckets of apples to our neighbors for a few pennies. Up the street beyond the Mortons was the home of my friend, Earnest Earl Sears. Next was the O'dells and beyond it the Oliver White home, one more home and then the woods going up on the knobs on which we often played.

To the west of us was the Shipper home with a son and daughter. They had a relative staying there often who drove a motorcycle. I remember how he was killed in a head-on accident with a car. Next door was the Jarboe family, who built a fine croquet court in their backyard which I often enjoyed. Then came the Wellborn family, home of Charles and Lucy. Behind it was a large barn in which we often played. One day, a donkey trapped us in the barn and we had trouble escaping. I got down and ran home, telling my folks that "one of those things Jesus rode has Sister trapped in the barn." Further across the alley was the home of the DeShazers. Mr. Ike had a small farm up the hill on Second Street with a barn and a team of mules, of great interest to us. His three children were Roberta, Alberta who married John Pullam, and Edgar, my seventh grade and high school teacher, who was my good friend. They were all great to us, and Bradley and I spent many hours in their home. Next door was Miss Mattie and on down the street the Cashman family. It was across Caldwell Street where the old cemetery was located in which we often played. And, across the street from our house was the big open field in which all the neighborhood kids spent many hours playing every kind of ball that we knew. To the east was the Morgan Caldwell home, with a large shaded lawn. Across the street were several homes including those of the Beauchamp family, good friends and members of our church. On down the street was the home of the Chapmans, our friends Homer and Owen who were outstanding football players. Further was the home of a family who had an outstanding basketball player, who in high school played for West End High

School in Nashville while I was at Vanderbilt. On down the west end of Second Street lived the Thurmond family, Hal and Brents. We loved their mother very much and their father, who was a funeral director and led the program for small boys, the Rangers. Then the homes of Garnett Franklin Felts and John Clark.

When I was eight or nine years old our family took a vacation trip into Tennessee. We drove to Nashville where we spent a short time. We went to the amusement park and rode the roller-coaster. Bradley was very young and he screamed the whole ride, scaring Mother and Dad for fear he might not be able to get his breath. We then went to Chattanooga and climbed what then seemed like a very steep hill up Signal Mountain.

I took piano lessens when I was very young but did not spend enough time practicing, so my parents gave up on me, something I regret, for I would love to be able to play the piano today. But later my teacher, Miss Hylda Richardson, asked me to join a group she was teaching violin. I enjoyed this very much and even acquired a used violin, but she taught us all she knew and the lessons ended. One year in High School they asked me to play the violin for a skit. I played a few lines before getting the gong that ended my violin career.

During the depression years there were few jobs for a young man. One of the first opportunities to make a little money came through my friend Talbott Mansfield. His father, Alderson Mansfield, was the press man at the News Democrat. This weekly newspaper normally printed twelve pages, which was the size of the large sheets they ran through the press. But often they would print 24 pages, which meant each sheet would print the other pages twice, and had to be separated. Talbot had the job of separating these pages Wednesday night and he paid me to help him at the rate of twenty-five cents each week. I was pleased to have this bit of extra money, but I also enjoyed the time at the newspaper office because the editor, Byrne Evans, was always at his desk those nights and would visit with us. Then I began to work for the florist, E. Weston Hamilton, delivering flowers on occasion. At first I took them on my bicycle, but after I became old enough to drive, I would deliver them in a car. I was especially busy at the time of dances delivering corsages, and at Christmas, Easter, Valentine's Day, Mother's Day, etc. The most lucrative job I had was during my junior year delivering special delivery letters for the Post Office. I met the mail several times a day and delivered specials before, during and after school. A special delivery stamp cost ten cents, and I received nine cents for each letter that I delivered. Sometimes this would mean several dollars a day, big money as long as it lasted. I made enough that winter to pay the cost of a trip to Washington, D.C. on the D.A.R. tour during spring break. There were several of us in the group chaperoned by our high school principal, Mr. Tanner. We went by train from Louisville spending several days seeing all the sights of our capitol. We saw all the monuments and national buildings, visited a session of Congress, saw the cherry trees which were in bloom at that time of year, and Mount Vernon. I took my box camera and have a great file of pictures of virtually all of the public buildings. One night I talked several of us into renting a cab to take us over the city at night. This was my first experience in leading a tour group. But I was not in favor with the parents of the girls when they found out about our impromptu excursion.

In High School I found great friends in H. T. Gill, son of the dentist, and John Brinson, whose father was Summers Brinson, pastor of the Methodist Temple. We all enjoyed making model airplanes and spent much time together. I was a part of the class of 1938 at Russellville High School. Included in that group were Charles Mac Noe, Lewis Watts, Bill Mack Richardson, George Willis, Martyne Brown who later married Pat Ryan, Sue Belle Hill, Lois Jean Fitzsimmons, Dorothy Ellen Frazier, Ollie Brown Hendley, Carolyn Mason, as well as H. T. and John. I played in the RHS band from the time of its beginning in our sophomore year. Ab Rhea and I were snare drummers. Ruth Thompson, who even in those years was a brilliant pianist, accompanied the band on the marimba. Bill Hite was a fine trumpet player who also directed a community band in which I played drums until finishing high school. One interesting experience I remember quite well was the night that President Franklin D. Roosevelt stopped to speak in Russellville. He was on a special train from Louisville with his friend Tom Rhea, and when it came through here he had it stop so that he could speak briefly from the rear platform. I was playing in our community band and was just down below him on the track when he spoke. This was July 8, 1938 and there were 6000 to 8000 people who heard him.

I spent much time at the typewriter, where I had won a medal in my freshman year. I worked on the newspaper, the Spizerinktum, both as a columnist and typing the copy for printing on the mimeograph machine. I also was editor of the annual, the Black and Gold, my senior year. We mimeographed the Black and Gold in the days before we were able to print a more ambitious annual. We made pictures of the members of our class and school activities, thirteen in all. We pasted them into each copy, which we sold for $1.00. I was too small to excel in athletics, but I was a cheerleader with Pat Ryan, Sue Belle Hill and Betty Hite. I played tennis often enough to become fairly good. I remember playing on the court on Seventh Street at the foot of the lot of the Goodwin family. We played with Hollis Goodwin, Sam Proctor and others of the family. Later I played often on the school court on Seventh Street at the end of what had been Logan College but by then must have been the Russellville Middle School. Later I played on the court on west Seventh Street on what was then part of the Bethel College property south of Gladish Court. I learned to play golf on the Russellville course. At that time ministers were given free membership so Bradley and I were able to play as often as we wished. Bradley became a much better golfer than I, but in later years I played often with him and Owen Chapman, both of whom were excellent, but they were nice enough to let me join them. I learned to swim in the rock quarry pond on the Hopkinsville Road and we often swam there and in the pool at old Logan College which was only open on special occasions. Bee Andrews often provided those opportunities and he occasionally conducted swimming and diving contests.

In high school and college Bradley and I often hitchhiked to Dunbar Cave near Clarksville to swim in the fine Olympic size pool there.

Russellville High School was small, probably no more than 150 students in the four years. There were just thirty-one in my graduating class of 1938. I was only sixteen when I graduated, for I had gotten ahead of my years. My folks thought I should have started to school a year earlier, so they had me take the second grade in the summer. I attended class all that summer at the home of Mrs. Seward on West Sixth Street. Then as we were finishing the seventh grade the teachers asked five of us to take the eighth grade in the spring and summer because they were afraid we would have too many in the class. So Ruth Everly, Jimmy Matherly, Ollie Brown Hendley and I started taking afternoon classes in the spring and into the summer so that we had passed every test that we would have been given in the regular term. As a result I was only twelve years old when I started high school. I was not at a disadvantage academically, but as I look back on it, I missed out on some things because of my youth that my brother Bradley was able to do because he was more mature at that stage.

I recall fine teachers all through school. Miss Fannie Bryan was my first grade teacher and she got me off to a good start. I read quite well even then. Mrs. Seward helped me through the second grade, but I missed some things because of the short time involved. Miss Mary Ermine Edwards helped me catch up in the third grade. Louis Williams was a fine teacher in the fifth grade who I admired very much. I was terribly upset when he was killed in a train accident a year later. He and Forest Duncan who both taught grade school classes were returning home from school one day when their car stalled crossing the L & N railroad. Mr. Duncan was able to escape, but Mr. Williams was killed. Mrs. Lewis Richardson, Miss Alfia, left a good impression on me in health and world events during the sixth grade. Edgar DeShazer was not only my seventh grade teacher but a good friend throughout my life. He and his sisters lived a block from us on Second Street. I spent much time in their home reading the newspapers with Bradley because we could not afford a daily paper. I often walked back from school events with him. And in later years when Mr. DeShazer had a high position in human resources in the state of Kentucky he helped me secure summer jobs for our girls during college.

We had some outstanding teachers in high school. Ruth Price not only gave me a good grounding in English composition and literature, but she produced fine plays, using the rather limited talent of a small school to great advantage. I owe Geneva Cornette a debt of gratitude for grounding me in typing, which I have used to great advantage throughout life. She also taught me shorthand, which I never used as well. But she and Ruth Price were two close friends who helped to mold our lives in high school. Together they sponsored the school paper, for which we produced typewritten copies each week. I spent much time typing copy.

Mrs. Tanner grounded us well in algebra and her son James Freeman Tanner was a fine teacher of geometry and American history. Mr. Tanner was also our principal. He was a good disciplinarian whom we called "Rod." We had Edgar

DeShazer for general science in which I did well. Miss Ruth Hall taught Latin for my first two years and she was succeeded by Virginia Miles Chaney, who often befriended me. Mary DeShazer was our librarian. I won the typing medal my freshman year, having learned to type rapidly and accurately, a skill that has helped me greatly throughout my life. In my junior year I won the DAR history medal, perhaps a portent of my majoring in history in college and eventually writing my portion of *The Story of Logan County*.

We had two good band directors, first Ben Sisk and then Bill Lukes under whom I played drums. Ab Rhea and I were the snare drummers during high school. Mr. Lukes introduced me to the tympani, or kettle drums as they were earlier known. He took me to Bowling Green one day for a quick lesson on the tymps which I played in rehearsal that afternoon and in the music contest piece at Western that Saturday. I never became very proficient on the tymps, but I later played them in musical events at Peabody College. Our band did very well in the regional contests, often receiving the highest ranking. Mrs. C. T. Canon, the wife of our superintendent, directed choral groups so I enjoyed singing in the men's glee club and the school chorus. One day in the spring of 1937 our band director Bill Lukes told me that we needed to have an alma mater for our school. He asked me if I knew any and I told him that the only one I knew was Vanderbilt's. I knew the words quite well since I was already a Vanderbilt fan. He liked the words and the tune was familiar. He thought that we should use it. We only changed two words and so we sang "Hail to thee our alma mater, Russellville all hail." To Vanderbilt, Bill Lukes and me, we owe our alma mater.

During my high school days I played my snare drum in a community band led by Bill Hite. We played for special occasions, at auction sales, and occasionally for political rallies. I remember one fall when we were taken by bus to every spot in the county where candidates were speaking. This meant we were out of school for the day and received lunch along the way. We were concluding one of these rallies at Dennis when it began to rain. I continued to play my drum and made a hole in the water-soaked head.

My cousin, Evelyn Long Briggs (later Mrs. Ed Riley), taught dance lessons for some time in the main room of the old Southern Bank of Kentucky. Lucy Linton played for her. Long invited Bradley and me to join her class and from there we began most enjoyable dances. We were taught tap and ballroom dancing. I remember doing a tap dance with Dorothy Ann Evans as toy soldiers. From the ballroom lessons grew a custom of outdoor dances at our friends' homes every week or so. We would dance on porches or driveways, usually to music by juke boxes. Occasionally we had dances at the Armory when we had visiting bands. One of these brought Little Johnny, the promoter for Phillip Morris—"Call…for… Phillip Morris!" We sometimes had cotillions which were very formal. Christmas dances were quite popular.

We had an outstanding group who did many things together during our high school years. Some twenty or more got together most every Friday night at one of our homes, more often than not at our home on Second Street. We would bring a few jars of cheese and crackers or other refreshments and spent much time visiting and dancing. We often gathered on Saturday nights to listen to the latest popular tunes on the Lucky Strike Hit Parade. One year we built a ping pong table on the second floor of our home and we all spent many hours improving our skills. We often went to other homes, and eventually Bessie Curd Nourse's father, Eugene Nourse, brought an old log cabin to the back yard of their home on Breathitt Street and erected a large room with open fireplace and hardwood floor which provided ample room for visiting and dancing. The group in these ruckuses as we called them, included Bessie Curd, Martyne Brown, Dorothy Ellen Frazier, Ruth Thompson, Lois Jean Fitzsimmons, Sue Belle Hill, Marion Joyce Berkman, Ollie Hendley, Ruth Everly, H. T. Gill, Paul Summers, John Brinson, Bill Mack Richardson, Charles Mac Noe, Lewis Watts, John Clark, Mickey McLaughlin and others. Lois Jean Fitzsimmons was my regular girl friend all through High School and to some extent during our college years. We were just automatically dating for most occasions. However, in those days I was not very romantic so about all we did was hold hands. This was not so for my brother who was quite a ladies man.

Several of us boys would sit in the city park swapping stories often till late in the night. One night we noticed a convoy of Army trucks coming into the square around the park. This was before the outbreak of World War II. They had obviously come from Fort Knox on their way to Mississippi for their summer training. The head of the convoy went around the park and out Fourth Street to the west. After a while there was a break and when the rest of the vehicles came to the park, they turned north toward the Lewisburg Road. Seeing what had happened, I said we should try to alert them to their mistake. So we jumped in my car and tore up around the convoy some miles before we were able to get their attention and tell them of their mistake. Then came great confusion as one by one each truck or other equipment pulled into a drive and backed out to head back to Russellville and the right road to join the rest of their contingent.

As I was growing physically in these early years, I was also maturing spiritually. I owe much of my religious philosophy to my parents. Mother and Dad were fine Christians long before my father entered the ministry. They had been active in their church and were good role models in the community. And they instilled in my sister. my brother and me a fine sense of right and wrong. They were especially warm toward members of every race. It was from them that I received my appreciation for others regardless of race or creed. One summer our church had an ice cream supper on the front lawn of the courthouse. While folks were being served I wandered inside to get a drink of water. To my surprise there were two fountains side by side, one labeled white and the other colored. I turned on the second to see what color it was. This was my early introduction to segregation.

I hardly knew what it was not to live in a preacher's home. So our life was centered in the church and in Dad's pastoral work. One fall when he was preparing for an evangelistic program, he asked the members of the church to take cards to suggest names of those we should invite to church membership. I took a card and to Dad's surprise my name was at the top of my list. Brother Hudspeth was preaching for a revival service in the church and one night I answered the call to accept Christ as my Savior. I think I was seven years old when my father baptized me in the baptistry of the Christian Church. I remember that night for I was very small and so lightweight that I bobbed in the water while waiting to be immersed in the name of the Father and Son and Holy Spirit. I was regular in Sunday School where I had some fine teachers--Mrs. Canon, Mrs. Ryan, and others. In those years I began to develop an ecumenical spirit because of the way in which my father led the congregation to participate in cooperative programs with the other churches of the community. He promoted union services in the summer on the lawn of old Logan College. And with other of his colleagues he organized vacation church school as a cooperative program of the downtown churches. Different age levels met at the various churches during this joint venture with a mass closing service at one or the other. As a result I often visited my Methodist friends or Baptists in BYPU. I learned to sing "A sunbeam, a sunbeam, Jesus wants me for a sunbeam.."

In the days before the Cub Scout program, you had to be twelve years old to become a Boy Scout. I had been a member of the Rangers, a group of young boys led by Brents Thurmond. But I wanted to be a Scout, so on my twelfth birthday I joined the Troop which met at the Methodist Church, where Walter Munday, the Methodist pastor, was Scoutmaster. I quickly learned the Scout Oath and Law and soon qualified as a Tenderfoot Scout. From there I passed the requirements for Second Class. With the encouragement of older Scouts like Hal Thurmond and Granville Clark I was soon a First Class Scout. I continued in Scouting by earning several merit badges. But somehow I never quite qualified as an Eagle Scout. I passed the required tests for Star Scout, but by that time the leadership had changed and I never actually received the badge. When I left home for Vanderbilt, I never managed to progress farther. I remember wearing my new uniform and badge to Scout Sunday in February soon after I became a Scout. Mr. Munday had an impressive service at the Methodist Church.

After the seventh grade, I spent several weeks with five other students who were asked to take summer work to pass on to the eighth grade. Just as I finished the course, I went to Scout camp, which was on the banks of the Mud River just above where it joins the Ohio River at Rochester. I had not been outside much until that time and I was delighted to have the chance to ride a boat on the river. But after two or three hours in the sun that day I was terribly sunburned. I had large burns on my legs which were quite painful the rest of the week in camp. When Mother and Dad came to see us on Saturday, bringing a large sack of bananas, I was glad to be able to go home with them, where I could recover from my burns. It was by far the worst sunburn I ever suffered.

When Walter Munday left, Dad became our Scoutmaster. He had had no previous experience, but he learned fast and did a great job. He took us to a camp on Drakes Creek near Bowling Green which was quite rustic but enjoyable. We took a man to cook for us and Mother handled the food. We spent lots of time in the water along with working on our Scout tests. I have a picture of the troop at attention in front of the camp. We were lined up by patrols. Bill Mack Richardson was the bugler and Pat Ryan is very much in evidence. Pat said where else could you get all you wanted to eat and have so much fun. The next year we went to another rustic camp near Glasgow. It was very similar and most fun. One day I took two members of my patrol to lay a trail for one of the tests. Crossing a field of high grass, Billy Clary was bitten by a snake. We immediately put all our Scouting skills to work. Bobby Clary made a tourniquet with a neckerchief and I cut two holes in the place where the bites were evident. We then squeezed out the offending poison as best as we could. Then I left the boys in the field while I ran like crazy back to camp to get help. I was really scared, but we were able to get Billy to a doctor and apparently he had no ill effects from the snake bite. We were in camp the summer that Ab Rhea's father, Tom Rhea, was running for Governor of Kentucky. Ab and I spent some time tearing down road signs for Mr. Rhea's opponent, Happy Chandler.

Our church had a fine summer conference program. For five years I spent a week each summer at the Kuttawa Springs Conference. Mother and Dad had taught in that conference and in later years I served as a counselor in the Kuttawa conference and the West Kentucky Chi Rho Camp. It was in an impressive friendship circle one night in my third year at the Kuttawa conference that I stepped forward in response to the invitation to those who would commit their lives to the ministry. From that night on my future was clear. Toward the close of my work in the Divinity School years later I was ordained in my church in Russellville. My father had led in planning it and my pastor presided. Dean John Keith Benton came from the Divinity School to present my credentials of preparation for the ministry. Elders from the Russellville church and the three churches I was serving as student pastor gave their approval. My spiritual life had found its culmination.

Some twenty-five miles from Russellville was well known Dunbar Cave, which many people had explored and enjoyed its wide mouth with a constant pleasant temperature. My grandmother had danced there in her younger days. In the 40s it was being developed as a tourist attraction. There was an excellent Olympic-size swimming pool, a lake with paddle boats, other recreation and a large cabin on one side of the lake. Dances became quite popular. Every Tuesday night a local band would play, and every Saturday there would be a large name band, like Tommy Dorsey, that attracted huge crowds to dance in the mouth of the cave. Bradley and I danced there many times and often would hitchhike to swim at the Cave. Mother was a fine Girl Scoutmaster and several summers she took her troop for a week at the clubhouse on the lake. Bradley and I accompanied them and ran errands while enjoying swimming in the pool. There was an area of spring water adjacent to the cave and Idaho Springs Hotel was quite popular for visitors wanting to drink the water and for excellent food. We occasionally went there for special group occasions. There were also springs and caves near Russellville. One small cave we explored from time to time and there was a large cave near Adairville. Diamond Springs on the Lewisburg road with its curative waters was attractive enough to warrant a hotel that lasted into the 40s. Kallebreate Springs and others were near Warren County. To the north Mammoth Cave was the central attraction of an extensive cave area. We often went there for trips through the cave and for meals at the hotel.

My grades were good enough to finish third in my class behind Lois Jean and Martyne. I represented our school each year in the district achievement tests, and I won the American History medal presented by the DAR. I made one of the speeches at commencement and was awarded a trophy for being named the most outstanding boy. And I received a reading certificate, recognizing four years of reading a required number of books. We had lots of fun in high school and were well prepared for entrance into college. Many of my friends left for prestigious schools as H. T. Gill and I entered Vanderbilt. I had been known as Sonny Coffman all through these years, but when I left for college, I told my folks they could call me anything they wished except for Sonny. They were quite helpful, so from that time on I was Ed Coffman, or some other nicknames.

My Parents – Edward (Pyke) and Emma Coffman

Aunt Lou, Uncle Tom and Aunt Lizzie Hill

Young Ed –
About Age 6

Young Emma Hill and Edward with Mother

Edward "Sonny" Coffman –
Teenager;
In My Russellville
High School Band Uniform

Bradley, Edward, and Emma Hill Coffman

Pyke and Emma

Tolbert Mansfield and
My Grandmother Julia Evans Coffman

2

Vanderbilt Years

I was very fortunate to be accepted at Vanderbilt. Their entrance requirements were very difficult and had I not looked ahead while in High School I might not have had the subjects they expected of incoming freshmen. H. T. Gill and I went together to Orientation and we roomed in old Kissam Hall. I went for fraternity rush week. After visiting several groups, I pledged Phi Kappa Psi, which had its own house at 2016 Terrace Place at the foot of the campus. I helped pay my expenses by serving the meals at the fraternity house.

My first courses at Vanderbilt included English, Chemistry, Trigonometry, Greek Mythology and history. Dr Edwin Mims opened my eyes to the wonderful world of English literature. As was his custom with every freshman class, he had us memorize Polonius' advice to Laertes:

"Come, my friends, 'tis not too late to seek a newer world;
Push off, and sitting well in order, smite the sounding furrows,
For my purpose holds to sail beyond the sunset
and the baths of all the western stars before I die
Though much has passed, much remains."

Little did I realize at the time, but this was a challenge to generations of Vanderbilt students which we all cherish to this day. Dr. Mims had us memorize some five hundred lines of poetry each quarter. I typed them up and in later years my fraternity brother, Bob Lodge and I mimeographed copies of them for succeeding classes. We sold them for a twenty-five cents. For the Shakespeare quarter Bob drew a cover with a picture that for all the world looked like Dr. Mims in Shakespearean pantaloons which we called Shakespeare's Shorts. We made sure we could recall the lines when we were back in Dr. Mims' classes.

I had some fine professors at Vanderbilt. Dr. Henry Swint taught some of my history courses in which I specialized. I had a most interesting course in Greek and Roman History for which I wrote a paper on the Parthenon, complete with pictures I made of the Parthenon in Nashville. My sophomore year I worked for Dr. Swint under the NEA program which paid students ten cents an hour to help professors who needed assistance. I worked long hours typing the manuscript of Dr. Swint's forthcoming book. From Dr. George Mayhew I learned much about comparative religion; I made an A for the three quarters of my senior year in the course for history majors. This enabled me to graduate with an A.B. degree cum laude in June of 1942.

I immediately joined the Vanderbilt Band in which I played all four years. The first year I played on my own snare drum from high school days. The second year the band was able to buy its own drums so I played on a gold colored instrument the next three years. On football game weeks we played downtown in Nashville at the main hotels, with cheer leaders stirring up enthusiasm for the games. Part of the fun was getting to play for out of town games. Our first trip was to Lexington for a game with the University of Kentucky. The morning we arrived our band filed in between rows of the fine UK band and it was a great thrill to look over and see former members of our High School band playing nearby--Charles Mac Noe, Bill Mack Richardson and others. We also played that fall in Birmingham for the Alabama game and Knoxville for the University of Tennessee battle.

One very interesting event took place in the fall when we were rehearsing on McGuggin Field. Francis Craig, who was a member of the radio station WSM staff orchestra, came to meet us with new music which he had just composed. It was the Vanderbilt fight song, Dynamite, and we played it that afternoon from his handwritten music. We did so well that we played it that Saturday game for the first time in public. This was the beginning of thousands of excited renditions of Dynamite at all Vanderbilt games I enjoyed playing it with the Vanderbilt band at a Homecoming many years later.

I also joined the Vanderbilt a cappella choir, which I enjoyed thoroughly. I well remember singing in Neely Auditorium for the Christmas concert when we did portions of The Messiah. We sang in old Ryman Auditorium with Dinah Shore, a former member of the Choir, who was giving a war support concert. And in the spring we took trips to Tennessee Tech in Cookeville, and other schools. Later we made more ambitious trips, singing at schools across Illinois to St. Louis, down through Tennessee to Memphis where we stayed at the Peabody Hotel when we sang

After Christmas my freshman year we went through hell week, an orientation for initiation in the Phi Kappa Psi fraternity. This included wearing of the VU freshman beanie, carrying a paddle for upperclassmen who desired to give us a few licks, and a night when we went through all sorts of indignities ending in being left alone on some road near Nashville to find my way home with no money and little else. But it was worth it when we were initiated into our fraternity which would be the home of our life for four years. I was honored that night with a Phi Psi ring which I wore proudly for many years for having the highest first quarter class average. I did all sorts of things for my fraternity, including wrestling in the intramural contests in my weight class which was very small. I actually won one match and took the other by default. Scott George was the member of my fraternity whom I most admired for his all-around ability academically and physically. Scott George, John Edge, Marcus Stubbs, Walter Jones, Walter Stone, H. P. Jones,

Bob Lodge, Clinton Wright, Elmore Hudgins, Homer Hoe, Rabbit Cordner and many others were fraternity brothers who I came to call good friends. My first year I was living in the dormitory but I took my meals at the house. Our cook we called Madame was a jolly person who knew us all well. We were well guarded by our house father, Uncle Frank Smith, a retired banker who lived in the house. We had many social events, including an annual formal dance at the fraternity house. Homecoming was a great week when we decorated our fraternity house and entered a float in the parade, all of which took many hours of work. In the summer of 1940 I went with two of my fraternity brothers to the Grand Arch Council of the Phi Kappa Psi fraternity at Spring Lake, New Jersey. We spent a day in New York at the World's Fair, then spending a night at the YMCA, I took the subway late on Saturday night to visit relatives in Greenwich Village. It was the first day I had ever been on a subway. I was house manager one year, which meant planning the meals and other business. My senior year I served as President of the fraternity.

In January of my freshman year my uncle Tom Hill died. He was like my grandfather, having helped rear my mother. I had been very close to him for he had taught me many things. As he grew older I learned to cut his hair and to shave him with a straight razor, something I never learned to do for myself. He was active in the Episcopal church and I had learned to appreciate its services as I went to church with him. It was a sad time for me when I came home for his funeral.

I worked at all sorts of jobs to help with my expenses while I was studying at Vanderbilt. I waited tables at my fraternity house to pay for my meals, collected laundry at my dormitory, Kissam Hall, sold mums downtown on college game days, and as mentioned, with my friend Bob Lodge edited a small booklet of poetry to be memorized by English students, selling it for twenty-five cents a copy.

In addition to my various jobs, I typed term papers for other students. I had my own typewriter in my room and being a fast typist I had a good volume of business. I charged ten cents a page and often typed term papers of some ten pages in length. I would charge $1.00 for a ten page paper and would throw in the title page and the bibliography. I once typed a chemistry thesis for a fraternity brother at thirty-five cents a page, including many lines of equations which had to be put in by India ink because of the critical markings which were not then available on most typewriters. During the depression one of the programs of the Roosevelt era was the National Youth Administration. It provided work for students who helped in the educational system. As noted, I worked in my sophomore year under the NYA program for Dr.. Henry Swint, typing the manuscript for the book he was writing. It paid ten cents an hour, not much, but more income than I had regularly that year. One summer when I was home from school I worked part time in the telegraph office in the lobby of the Kaintuck hotel. I received and delivered telegrams and sent telegrams to the office in Bowling Green.

In my sophomore year our fraternity pledged Clinton Wright, who became my roommate at the house and lifelong friend. We visited each other in the summers and I came to know his mother who lived in Chattanooga. She often brought us homemade cookies which were a real treat. Clinton entered Med School and he met a young woman from England, Ruth, who had come to Vanderbilt to study medicine during the War. When they decided to get married, I went with them to Chattanooga to act as father of the bride since it was impossible for her parents to be there. After the wedding, I wrote them about the ceremony, telling them the church was beautifully decorated with roses and greens, by which I meant the background foliage. They didn't understand this, thinking I meant they used green vegetables. Before graduating Clinton and Ruth had a baby which they proudly came to show my parents. It was always a joke in our family about the way they bathed little M.D. on their dining room table.

I had little athletic ability especially of a college level, but I wanted very much to win a V to wear on my sweater. So I did my best to win one as manager of one of the college teams. I tried it at track, tennis and basketball. I did quite well with the basketball team and should have been made manager except that my competitor was a fraternity brother of the captain, so he got the job. Eventually Jim Buford, who coached several teams, knew how I had tried. He called me in one day to see if I would be the manager of the golf team. I was delighted, even though it was not very demanding. But before I graduated I proudly wore a V on my sweater. The only thing I did athletically was to represent my fraternity in the intramural wrestling tournament. I was small but wiry. I won my first match and then a second by default when my opponent did not show. This was the extent of my athletic achievement in college.

In addition to these many extra-curricular activities, I was also in the Ace Club and Owl Club (both scholastic honoraries).

Vanderbilt had gym dances in the old gymnasium every Saturday night. They were free and we all enjoyed them. Usually they didn't involve dates, but twice a year we had Junior and Senior Proms when big name bands were brought in for weekends. There would be a formal dance on Friday night, a tea dance Saturday afternoon and an informal dance that night. I often had dates for these times, most often Elaine Vincent, who lived in Nashville and was a student at Ward-Belmont. She was a cousin of Martyne Brown and I had known her before going to Vanderbilt. The Vincents were quite nice to me, sometimes having me over for a meal, and her father took me to a ball game occasionally. While she was at Ward-Belmont we often went to dances there which were quite formal. However, we were never allowed to leave at intermission. They opened the dining room so we had refreshments at the school. The mansion which was the main building of Ward-Belmont is now the central building of Belmont College. Of course I had no car at school, but occasionally I would rent a car for special occasions so we had time to go out for refreshments. One night we pulled up to the ice-cream parlor Candyland and spotted two men inside robbing the store. We called the police and waited breathlessly till they appeared and caught the men inside the store. Needless to say, we had no ice cream there that night.

Early Life and Family

Ryman Auditorium was the home of the Grand Old Opry, but it was also the center of many cultural events. Students were encouraged to work as ushers for events, which included grand opera, light opera, symphony orchestras and such plays as Helen Hayes in *The Corn Is Green*. You could enjoy them without cost. As a result I was able to see great plays, enjoy many light operas and several full operas. I remember enjoying the Navy Band and other outstanding musical groups. One spring I saw the very first Steeplechase in Nashville, which became an annual event. And I saw a benefit golf match by two of the top pro golfers in the country, perhaps one was Ben Hogan.

Vanderbilt years were good years, leaving many good impressions and experiences and litany of lifelong friends. I studied hard and made good grades, eventually graduating cum laude. I received my degree in 1942. By this time I had already enrolled in the Divinity School.

Edward and Bradley with Mother and Father

The Vanderbilt Band – Edward is third from right

Phi Kappa Psi Fraternity – Edward in second row, second from left

Bradley and Edward in front of house on Seventh Street

Ed in Downtown Nashville

3

Seminary Years and the Beginning of Ministry

I finished my undergraduate years as the country was at war. I had planned to become a minister so I had already made plans to enter seminary for my theological studies. The United States recognized a need for ministers so provision was made for students who were studying for the ministry to be classified as V8, which meant they were able to continue their studies. I fully intended to become a chaplain, so I prepared to continue my schooling for this purpose. Earlier, I had applied to Divinity Schools at Vanderbilt, the University of Chicago and Yale. I was accepted at all three schools. In fact the Disciples Divinity House at Chicago offered me a most attractive financial opportunity, much better than either Vanderbilt or Yale. But because of the war situation, I felt it was best to stay at Vanderbilt where I had already taken some courses needed by the Divinity School there.

When I enrolled in the fall of 1942 I made plans to live at the Disciples House at 2005 Grand Avenue in Nashville. This was to be my home for the next two years as I pursued my studies and entered into the beginning of ministry. It was an excellent facility for the Disciple students in the Divinity School. We did many things together and had a monthly dinner meeting when we often had visiting ministers or missionaries share their experiences with us. The building served as the office and home of the Christian Church in Tennessee. Dr. and Mrs. W. P. Harmon, the State Secretary, lived on the first floor which included a large living area behind the state offices. There were four apartments for married couples plus rooms for visitors on the second floor. Single students lived on the third floor. My first roommate was Tweedy Foster, with whom I developed a close friendship. After he graduated, Tweedy went to the Christian Church in Cullman, Alabama, where I visited him on several occasions and later was in his wedding to Lilly. My second year at the house my roommate was Carnie Burcham of Galax, Virginia, a graduate of Lynchburg College. We became very close friends and I went to Alabama to be the best man in his wedding. We were together several times in Chi Rho Camps which he directed, and through the years at church conventions. Claylon Weeks was one of the single students, who while we were still in school married Helen Mitchell who had been the Secretary to Mr. Harmon in the state office. From Vanderbilt they went into missionary training for the Disciples and spent many years in the Belgian Congo. Neal and Sarah Wyndham were also a couple on the second floor. Others on the third floor included Charles Harrison. Also we had several students from other denominations in the house, mostly Methodists who had no foundation house as did we.

In 1992 a group of those who had been together in the Disciples House in the 1940s started a custom of reunions each summer. We often used a condo in Pigeon Forge, Tennessee and later used our national conference grounds at Christmount in Black Mountain, North Carolina. Those left of our group when we gathered at Christmount in 2006 were Helen and Claylon Weeks, Nina and Preston Parsons, Sarah and Neal Wyndham, Leon Berry, and Carol and I. If we were all still able, we planed to have another reunion at Penny Farms in Florida in 2007. But by that time several of us were not well, so we never met again. Sarah Wyndham died in September of 2008 and Neal is in an Alzheimer's hospital.

The faculty of the Divinity School while I was there included some very fine professors to whom I owe much credit for my preparation for the ministry. Dr. John Keith Benton was Dean and professor of church history. Dr. Robert M. Hawkins was the creative professor of New Testament who taught us how to use the Bible. Dr. Philip Hyatt was an outstanding professor of Old Testament, who shared the work he was doing for his parts of the forthcoming Interpreters Bible which has been for many years one of the best commentaries available. I did well in theology under Dr Burroughs, but I got a long overdue term paper without which I could not graduate, in the last day of school. Dr. Campbell, the representative of the Congregational Church on the Divinity School faculty, taught homiletics, and gave us an insight into the spirit of the pastorate as well as sermon preparation. Dr. Harmon taught the Disciples courses on history and polity of our denomination. I never had courses in seminary with Dr. George Mayhew, who had taught my undergraduate courses in comparative religion, but he was probably the originator of the Disciples House and my good friend with whom I sometimes played tennis. I also played ping pong often with Dr. Hawkins. We had regular chapel services each week, where I became familiar with the worship practices of the Methodist church, which dominated life at the Divinity School.

The Divinity School had a close relationship with Scarritt College. We could take courses in either school with no difficulty. I took advantage of Scarritt for courses in American church history and Christian Education. I was especially fortunate to have a course in hymnody under Dr. Charles Washburn from whom I gained much appreciation for the great hymns of the church. He was the music leader for Scarritt, producing fine musical programs in the chapel. His friend Richard Thomason was the organist. But along with it I became a close friend of "Uncle Charley" Washburn, for whom I often drove his car and who was a great inspiration to me long after my school days.

I found a friend in these days, Jean Ward, with whom I studied many evenings and sometimes dated. I also had friends in the girls at Scarritt College, one of the most interesting was Nickie Courier.

In the fall of my first year in seminary I was asked to serve as choir director and leader of the youth program at the Eastside Christian Church. I went to the church by bus for choir practice, youth groups and worship services. I was a novice at it all, but got a good start on what would be my life work. Soon I was asked to supply for several nearby churches. My first sermon was at the Bells Christian Church in what later became the Bellevue area of Nashville. I sometimes supplied for friends needing someone to fill in. I remember being asked by my good friend, Mrs. Carl Chaney, to come preach one Sunday at Tullahoma, Tennessee, where many years later Connie and Ed were members and I was asked to preach by their good pastor Don McLaughlin. And occasionally I was asked to lead the singing for revivals which my fellow students were holding. The one I remember best was a two week, twice a day revival at Carthage, Tennessee, where George Holwager was pastor. By that time I was preaching for student churches so I had to make hurried trips on weekends to preach elsewhere. We had no musical instrument, so I led all the music on my own. But between services George and I found time to do some fishing on the Cumberland River. I later discovered that Carthage was the home of Al Gore, who served two terms as Vice-President of the United States and lost a closely contested election as President to George W. Bush. I had a course with him at the Divinity school when I was working on my doctorate. He and his parents were all distinguished alumni of Vanderbilt.

In the fall of 1942 I was asked to preach one Sunday at a small Christian Church near Nashville's Bellevue section. I asked Dad for help with my sermon and he suggested a text which I might use. It was Saturday before time for church and I spent long hours struggling to come up with a sermon. I was so afraid that I wouldn't remember what to say that I typed out every word, including the Lord's Prayer. I slipped off that morning to take a bus to the church, afraid that my fraternity brothers might discover me and come to hear me preach. .

In June of 1943 I agreed to serve the Christian Church at Daysville, Kentucky once a month. Then I was asked to serve another Sunday a month at the Bethlehem Christian Church near Madisonville in Hopkins County, Kentucky, and a third Sunday a month at the Sinking Fork church near Hopkinsville, Kentucky. This meant regular trips by bus or train. In some cases, when there were night services or revivals, it meant being away for long weekends. I often spent the night with families in my churches or had meals with them on Sundays. I was very eager to have as many programs as possible, so I often arranged to have special services at Christmas, Easter and other times. I remember many families in each of these congregations. When we had night services at the Daysville church, it was always by coal oil lamps since there was no electricity in the church. We had a very successful revival at Bethlehem when we had five girls join the church.

At Daysville the Adams family were especially nice to me and often had me for Sunday dinners. Mr. Adams was Superintendent of the Sunday School and led the singing with great enthusiasm. I enjoyed singing in the choir. His daughter Mae was a fine organist on the old fashioned pump organ. She has been my friend through the years and always joins us at church in Russellville today. Her brother Bill became a good friend and his was the first wedding I had in my ministry. Bill is active today as an elder in the Bowling Green Christian Church. The Gordon family lived just two doors from the church and the Utleys across the road. It was at Daysville that I had my first funeral. Actually, Dad and I had it together, but it was the beginning of many, many funerals throughout my ministry. We had several revivals at Daysville. It was also at Daysville that I had my first baptism. I baptized one or two boys in a creek about a mile from the church. It was also at Daysville that I had my first special worship services. I worked out a Christmas service that combined scripture and music, with a mimeographed program. Mae told me that it was a little ambitious for their congregation, but I persisted and we had a very worshipful Christmas celebration.

At Bethlehem there were several Jackson families with whom I spent much time. There were five brothers, several of whom lived in Madisonville, and were fine leaders when I was later pastor there. Martin Hanner was a big farmer and miner who always built the fires before church at Bethlehem. The Hanner family often had me stay with them over weekends and fed me royally. We had a very successful revival one summer and I baptized five girls in Pond River. Mr. Hanner warned me about the water moccasins he had seen in that creek the day before. He asked me several times if I was sure I wanted to baptize in the water there. I knew he was kidding me, but I was very cautious the first time I stepped into the water at Pond River. Many years later I met one of those girls who was by then married to Floyd Brown the principal of Madisonville-North Hopkins High School. In his office one night before a school service where I was preaching, he asked me if I knew his wife. When I started to say no, she interrupted and told me that she had been one of the five girls I had baptized in Pond River long years ago. Wilma later became a member of P.E.O. in Madisonville and I saw her at the state convention in Lexington not long before Carol became ill. The Hanners' daughter Louise later was a strong supporter of my ministry in Madisonville.

The Superintendent of the Sunday School at Sinking Fork was my good supporter. I stayed with several families there, one of whom had two boys about my age who enjoyed taking me for rides around Pennyrile State Park. Once I double-dated with the pastor of the Sinking Fork Baptist Church. My times with the congregations I served as a student minister were most satisfying and paved the way for my future full-time ministry.

In the fall of 1942 Bradley was having a good year as quarterback for the Russellville High School football team. I did my best to get home to see him play on Friday nights and went to most out-of-town games. I would hitchhike to wherever they were playing and was able to see him in a very successful year. I

Seminary Years and the Beginning of Ministry

also hitchhiked at times to the churches I was serving on weekends. One time I was leaving Russellville for Madisonville and a Bowling Green-Hopkinsville bus picked me up. It was driven by a good friend Winkie Sosh, who worked for the company and was deadheading the bus to Hopkinsville. I told him that I needed to stop at the Daysville Christian Church to pick up my Bible and sermon notes I had left there the Sunday before. He pulled the bus over to the side of the road and waited for me to go into the church on my errand.

At Christmas time in my seminary years I worked at the Post Office, giving me good money for the coming year.

During this time while I was still in the Divinity School and serving my student churches Dad gave me many opportunities to became involved in the larger working of our denomination. We attended the State Convention of the Christian Church in Kentucky at Frankfort and other area activities. In 1944 Mother, Dad and I went to Columbus, Ohio, for the International Convention of the Christian Church, Disciples of Christ. We stayed in Columbus with the family of Louise Walker and thoroughly enjoyed our week. Dr. Clarence Lemmon was serving as President of the Convention. He was well known in our church as an outstanding preacher and author. Because of his somewhat liberal views, Dr. Lemmon was attacked at the convention by a conservative group who denounced him with a full page ad in the Columbus paper that was on sale at the front entrance to the convention the night he gave his presidential address. Two years later it was at the convention again in Columbus that I first met Dr. Lemmon, which would set the direction of my later ministry. While in Columbus that year we saw a football game at Ohio State which had an outstanding All-American. There were some 90,000 people at the game, which seemed almost unbelievable in comparison to our Vanderbilt crowds which at that time seldom exceeded 30,000.

On my last day in the Divinity School I was quite busy finishing up some papers before completing my work At 6:00 o'clock on a Friday night I put the last of those papers under the door of my professor and caught a 7:00 o'clock train to Chicago. After an all night ride, I left Chicago to meet Nikkie Courier who had been a friend at Vanderbilt and was finishing a summer of work at Garrett Theological Seminary on the campus of Northwestern in Evanston. She was leaving that night for her home in Paris, Tennessee. Her uncle was Dr. Barnett Blakemore who had been Dean of the Disciples House at the University of Chicago. He remembered me because he could not understand why I had not accepted the scholarship he had offered me to the Disciples Divinity House. Nikkie and I had a delightful day seeing the sights in Chicago and had lunch at the Sheraton Hotel. I put her on the train that evening and spent the night at a fleabag hotel before going by train the next morning to Lake Geneva, Wisconsin for a week at the United Christian Youth Movement conference. This was the second week I had spent there while in seminary and I had made good friends. Several of them were from Chicago and they took me home with them when the conference ended. I stayed at their home and went with them to their church the next morning. But the night before, we went dancing at the Trianon, a famous dance hall where Lawrence Welk, with his Champagne Music was playing.

During my first year in seminary I began to apply for acceptance in the military as a chaplain. I could not be accepted in the Army because I was under the minimum age of twenty-four. So I looked to the Navy which had no such requirement. I was first turned down because I was sixteen pounds under the minimum weight. So for months I did everything I knew to gain weight. I swam and played basketball at the gym almost daily, ate two cakes of yeast and drank two quarts of milk a day. But I never gained more than fifteen pounds. In February of 1944 I went to Cincinnati, Ohio to take a test for acceptance as a candidate for second lieutenant which was needed for preparation for the chaplaincy. But I was sent home because I had a history of asthma, and the doctor had detected a heart murmur. I went back to Russellville where two doctors both said they could determine no heart murmur. But when I returned to Cincinnati the doctor still claimed he could hear the murmur. So I was rejected by the Navy. One day in Nashville I passed a recruitment office for the Marines. I told the doctor my story and when he examined me, he said he saw no reason to reject me and accepted my application for a commission. I was told to be ready to report to New Orleans at any time. But after six months I had heard nothing. When I requested my status, I was told that I would not be called. The only thing that I could figure was that the war was coming to an end and they knew chaplains would not be needed. So why should I be given a commission and sent to chaplains school.

After learning my fate with the military, I continued serving my three student churches until the spring of 1945. Miller Dungan was leaving the Christian Church at Leitchfield, Kentucky about fifty miles from Russellville. He asked me to come visit and soon I accepted a call as pastor of the Leitchfield church and began my first full-time ministry. I very much enjoyed my year in Leitchfield. I was young and well educated which meant that I was asked to do many things in the community as World War II was coming to a close. One of my first involvements was helping arrange and conduct a community prayer service in celebration of the close of the European phase of the war. I received many invitations to meals and special events. I was soon busy learning to prepare sermons, preaching twice on Sunday's, leading prayer meeting, teaching the youth Sunday School class and leading the youth group. The church had a small parsonage which I furnished mostly with things from home, especially the living room and bedroom. I was soon asked to substitute in classes at the high school, which I was happy to do. I was asked to help with the Boy Scout troop and became in reality the Scoutmaster, although the chairman of the committee actually had the title. I spent many hours in troop meetings and training of the boys. I took them on several overnight hikes to a nearby cabin. And we went to Council jamborees and other competitions. Most amazing was the fact that I was asked to sponsor two different 4-H groups even though I had had no experience in 4-H. But our groups did well. I took them to regional competition for which I had to train them. To my surprise one of them

Seminary Years and the Beginning of Ministry 33

won first place for animal judging that I had helped them prepare. I attended all the basketball games, even going with the team for most of its out-of-town games. Leitchfield had a good team that year so I was appreciated for my support.

But my popularity came to a halt, at least to a degree, at Halloween. A young couple who ran the dining room at the hotel announced that they would be open that night, hoping to avoid some of the destruction of past years. I thought this was a fine gesture and told my congregation so. That night after prayer meeting I invited two couples to go with me to the hotel and we visited there for half an hour. There were lots of activities, but in one corner several young people had brought a record player and were dancing. I took no notice of it but having danced all my life it did not bother me. But there were others who were very disturbed by dancing. The next morning I was the talk of the town for having been to that Halloween party. The Methodist minister, who had been quite friendly, told me I had ruined what he was trying to do in the community. And on Sunday the Baptist minister announced that he had changed his sermon and preached on the evils of dancing and my approval of it. This created concern on the part of the chairman of my board whose wife was a strong Baptist. But others complimented me for what I had done unknowingly. One of them was the sister of the chairman of the board. As a result I felt my ministry was no longer effective, but I continued to serve as best I could.

In the fall I had been invited to come to the Grapevine Christian Church near Madisonville to preach for a revival. We had good crowds with much interest on the part of the young people, several of whom had known me while I was on the faculty of the Kuttawa summer youth conference. While I was there I had a call from my brother Bradley who asked me to meet him and Margaret Dorris to marry them. I met them in the office of the Madisonville church. I was surprised that they had a license, for Margaret's parents, Judge and Mrs. Homer Dorris, did not want her to get married until she had graduated from high school. She was then in her junior year at Olmstead High School. I never knew just how they got a license without Jurdge Dorris' consent, but I knew they were going to get married and so I was pleased that they wanted me. I married them in the office at Madisonville while a young man in the church played the organ upstairs and with another young man witnessing the wedding. As soon as the service was over, I had them call Margaret's parents to tell them that they had been married. I then gave Bradley and Margaret money for a wedding dinner and the keys to my parsonage in Leitchfield where they spent their honeymoon. This was the beginning of a beautiful marriage that lasted until Bradley died five years later. And it was also the beginning of a very cordial friendship with the Dorrises. After young Bradley was born, he was very fortunate to have two good sets of grandparents who gave him much love and support as he was growing up.

One family in the Leitchfield church was especially nice to me. Mrs. Jones, her daughter, and her granddaughter Patsy Poole, often invited me to meals. I thoroughly enjoyed their good food and friendship. They often invited me to go places with them in their nice car. But I began to realize that they were trying to get me to take a special interest in Patsy. She was our church organist, and worked at the bank. I enjoyed being with her, but had no matrimonial interest. I was coming home from a meal at their house about ten o'clock one night, walking past the Methodist Church. As I stepped up on my porch, I heard the fire siren and looked back where I had just come and saw the top of the Methodist Church in flames. I rushed back and helped to move some of the things from the church office, but most of the sanctuary was already burning. I stayed that night until the fire was over. Sometime that evening the tower burned and we heard the large church bell fall. Later they had the bell melted down and made small souvenir replicas as a money-raising project. After I had moved to Mayfield, they sent me a bell in appreciation for my help that night. It is a good momento of my year in Leitchfield.

The furor over the Halloween party never died out completely, so in June of 1946 I was pleased to accept an invitation from the First Christian Church of Mayfield, Kentucky, to join them as director of Christian Education. We had an excellent youth program that summer. I took them to summer conference and a few to the national United Christian Youth Conference at Lake Geneva, Wisconsin. My friend, C. A. Byrne, whom I had known from summer conference days was a good supporter, as were several others. I acted as sponsor for the district youth program that summer, and it was through my contact with Mr. Martin, the pastor of the Christian Church in Paducah, that I was contacted by Dr. C. E. Lemmon who was looking for an associate to direct the college program at the First Christian Church in Columbia, Missouri. The Paducah pastor had told him about me and this resulted in my first contact with the man who was to become my senior minister and my mentor through the rest of my life He invited me to visit Columbia and after a brief visit with the leaders of the church I was called to my first major ministry.

Mother, Bradley, Grandmother Julia, and Dad

Relaxing in the Living Room of house on Seventh Street with
Mother and Grandmother

4

Columbia, Missouri

In the middle of September, 1946, I loaded my Ford car which I had bought the previous spring in Leitchfield. I drove to Columbia, Missouri, arriving just before a Family Night Dinner, where I was introduced and asked to tell of my background. This was the beginning of my first of three major pastorates. It would last twelve years and completely changed the nature of my ministry and family life.

When I arrived in Columbia, Dr. and Mrs. C. E. Lemmon invited me to stay in their home at 200 Thilly Avenue. They often rented rooms to college students and I found myself living there for three years in Columbia until I was married. There were two law students who also lived there in my first years, Jim Craig and Gerald Hawkins. Later Jack Hunter was in one of the rooms and we became good friends. My ministry was of a dual nature. I was the Associate Minister of the First Christian Church and had some responsibility for the youth program of the church. And I always helped lead the worship services of this very large congregation. This was an excellent learning experience, for Dr. Lemmon was an authority in church organization and from him I acquired many skills that I would use throughout my life. We shared the joys of great worship and the responsibilities of good pastors. Over coffee at Ernie's across the street from the church we often compared sermon ideas and programs for the life of an active congregation. To my father and to Dr. Lemmon I owe much of whatever pastoral skills I may have acquired.

The other side of my responsibility in Columbia was working with the large number of Disciple students on the three campuses at the University of Missouri, Stephens College and Christian College (now Columbia College). I was called to direct the program of campus ministry for a church that had long recognized its opportunities to serve college students. In those days I was known as a student worker, but today we would call it campus ministry. I inherited a well organized program which it was my privilege to serve for twelve years. The Christian Student Congregation involved students from all three schools. We were organized like a small congregation, with officers, committees, a budget, and a weekly mimeographed paper, the *CSCer*. I had an office from which I worked with the group and met with students daily. When I first went to Columbia that office was on the upper floor of the Bible College on the University campus. There were two rooms with a larger lounge area and an inner office. We were in the working area of the Bible College and under the oversight of the Dean, then Dr. Lhamon. He frowned on bridge playing but we had a card table, which his granddaughters who were then in CSC had provided as a "small folding table." Later my office was moved downtown to the church, making it more central to the three schools. We were actually a part of the operation of the First Christian Church and acted under the Student Work Committee, which served as my board. It was an outstanding group of educators, including Dr. Jack Matthews, Dean of Students at the University, William Bedford of the music department at Christian College, Mary Omer of Stephens College, Dr. Thomas Shrout, Dean of the Bible College, Max Schwabe, a state representative in the state of Missouri, and five or six others from the congregation.

We had a CSC Sunday School class each week which I usually taught. On Sunday evenings we had a large gathering in the social hall that included a light supper prepared and served by the students themselves, group singing, a worship service and good programs by visiting speakers. They were often from the colleges, but also included community leaders. After the program we would push back the tables and dance for an hour or more. In the days after the War this attracted large numbers of students. We normally had a hundred to a hundred and fifty at our CSC Sunday evening programs.

We often had skits and fun programs which the students organized for entertainment. Together we participated in activities on the three campuses which involved students from our group.

At the beginning of each semester we prepared an attractive brochure inviting students of the three schools to our church services and the CSC program. We had some 2500 Disciple students in attendance at the three schools, so this was no small endeavor. We were able to secure the names of most of those students from the schools and distributed invitations as well as possible. Occasionally we printed posters advertising our programs. Throughout the year we had some special series such as our popular Courtship and Marriage Clinic for which we invited outstanding speakers who attracted much interest.

Twice a year we had Retreats at the Lake Ozark State Park. We rented several cabins which surrounded a lodge with assembly hall, dining room and kitchen. We chartered busses to carry seventy-five to a hundred students who normally spent the weekend at the Retreat. The students prepared and cooked the meals. We had an attractive program for the weekend, including the topics of the speakers, morning devotions and worship services. We usually invited some well known minister to be our speaker. Throughout the years they have included some very fine leaders of our brotherhood. The weekend included swimming and boating in the Lake of the Ozarks, touch football, volleyball, softball games and hiking. We closed each evening with a meaningful friendship circle, often around a campfire. We always had adult sponsors at the retreats. Some of them included Tom and

Mildred Shrout, Sue and Ken Davis, Don and Thelma Brooker, and others. The fall and spring retreats were highlights of our CSC year. We always ended each evening, as we did our regular Sunday night program by singing "Spirit of the living God, fall afresh on me, melt me, mold me, fill me, use me; Spirit of the living God, fall afresh on me."

CSC had elaborate Christmas dinners to which we invited the Student Work Committee and other leaders of the church. Dr. Lemmon was always a highlight of the evening, a time he enjoyed making fun of my foibles. In the years when I was living at their home we had difficulty parking in the drive. He often told of the fact that I was always the last one to come in at night. In the spring we had a graduation dinner when we honored the seniors who would be leaving and awarded several special honors. For this time we printed a fine program which listed the active members of CSC and recalled the major events of the year. This was done in a very attractive way and became a valued memento of the year.

We had some outstanding leaders in CSC during the years I was there. The president each semester spent much time organizing and leading the group. These were a fine group who remain warm in my memory. The president one summer session was a university student Carol Jean Alexander, who soon became my wife and joined me in very fine direction of the CSC program. One of her early talents was the planning of the evening meals. She became so proficient at it that she soon was asked to plan and serve meals for groups of four hundred or more being served by the church. When we were married, the CSC presidents all served as ushers for our wedding. One of these was Bob Simpich, who was a fine artist. We were involved in his wedding and later often visited Bob and Janice at Colorado Springs, where they taught for years and still maintain an amazing business producing beautiful character dolls. Among our treasures today are the Christmas carolers they make which grace our living room each year. Ray Rowland was for years the editor of the *CSCer,* known for his wit, who in later years became a professor of journalism at St. Cloud University in St. Joseph, Minnesota. Glenn Geiger often used his talents at grilling chickens on the way to becoming a professor in the College of Agriculture at the University of Missouri. Glenn met Dolores Quick washing dishes after CSC meals, one of many marriages that had their beginnings in our student group. Glenn and Dolores were our close friends and remain so today. We visit them in Columbia each year and often at their apartment in Pensacola, Florida. Eldon Drennan, who became a minister in the Christian Church, succeeded me as director of the Christian Student Congregation. Bob Leach is still a very active leader in the Columbia church. Through the years I married several of these CSC couples, among them Nelson and Lorene Trickey, who recently invited us to the celebration of their fiftieth wedding anniversary.

During my years in Columbia I participated in all the national conferences of student workers. And as Parker Rossman organized national student conferences, we always took large delegations. Many of those were held at Estes Park, Colorado or Lake Geneva, Wisconsin. Carol and I enjoyed these especially as our children were growing up, for we could take them with us for delightful vacations. As the leader of the largest campus organization in the Christian Church in Missouri, I naturally took a lead in the organization of the Missouri Disciple Student Fellowship. We had several state conventions in Columbia, Springfield, Kirksville, and Warrensburg. We also had a number of spring retreats for the state group at the Lake of the Ozarks.

The churches in Columbia with campus ministry programs worked together in the Students Religious Council. Together we worked for the total religious life of the campuses. I worked actively in SRC with many fine students from other groups and through it became friends of their directors. John Clayton, the fine leader of the Westminster Foundation, Warren Briggs of the Wesley Foundation, and the leader of the Congregational/Evangelical Chapel. I became friends of the Jewish program, Hillel, and often spoke to them.

Another cooperative program was the annual Religious Emphasis Week on the three campuses. This was a national program which brought outstanding speakers each year for a week of lectures, classroom presentations and worship services. Jim Stoner was the national director of this program and he worked with us in Columbia for most of the years I was there. We had some very effective Weeks and attracted favorable comments from the administrators of the schools. Jim asked me at times to participate in similar programs at other schools and I had good times in Warrensburg, Kirksville, the University of Arkansas, and other campuses. While I was at Fayetteville, Arkansas, I was approached by the First Christian Church to consider coming as their pastor. I was very tempted but decided I should stay in Columbia. I have often wondered how our life might have changed had we become Arkansans.

In the fall of 1947 the International Convention of the Christian Church was held in Buffalo, New York. I took Mother and Dad with me for the week at the convention. We enjoyed Niagara Falls and then we headed east for a long trip home. Our first stop was at East Aurora, New York where we visited the Roycroft Inn of Elbert Hubbard, a leader of an experimental group of whom Dad had read. Then east across upstate New York to Boston and down to New York City. While there we saw the first cast of "Oklahoma", in its second year on Broadway. Then down to Richmond through Virginia and to Wilson, North Carolina to visit Dad's brother Selby before returning home.

I had many good friends among the students in CSC. Many of them were veterans just back from the War and just about my age. Larry Muir, Rex Olsen, Glenn Geiger, Jack Hunter and others often participated in campus activities together, sharing meals and recreation. Mrs. M. M. Slaughter, mother of Charlotte Slaughter in CSC, took an interest in us and often had us for meals. Martha Burton, secretary of our church, became a friend of many of us, befriending us with goodies and meals. We included many girls in our activities and I occasionally dated a few of them.

But I became aware of one especially who my friends told me was particularly interested in me. After spending some time with Carol Jean Alexander, I finally asked her for a date. We went to dinner at Harwell Manor, a fine restaurant south of the University campus, one evening in June of 1948. And that was the beginning of a torrid romance. I had had several good friendships through the years—Lois Jean in high school, Elaine in college, Jean Ward and Nikkie Courier in seminary. But they were always platonic relationships. I was not amorous, as was my brother, and as Mother later told Carol when we became serious. That soon changed, and for a year we were very close. At Christmas I took Carol home to Russellville where she was warmly received by Mother and Dad. And we enjoyed good times with Bradley and Margaret. That relationship continued to grow until in March the next spring Carol and I announced our engagement one Sunday evening in Morris Parlors after CSC, with Carol's folks, Frank and Lenora Alexander. This created quite a sensation in the church and we were entertained with many parties until we were married in the First Christian Church on Sunday, June 5, 1949. Dr. Lemmon and Dad married us in the presence of an overflow crowd of 900 church members, friends and students. Dr. William Bedford played the organ, Mary Alice Bedford and Bill Phillips sang. Betty Ann Dysart was Carol's maid of honor, with Dolores Quick, Sabra Gordon, Betty Jo Dunkeson .and her cousin, Rita Alexander serving as bridesmaids. Bradley was ill and not able to come, so Carney Burcham was my best man. Don Pittenger, Bob Dunkeson, and others were groomsmen. Linda Lewis was the flower girl and Mark Hale the ring bearer. The sanctuary was crowded when over 900 came to see their young minister and his lovely bride, who was their favorite, commit their vows to each other. The Christian Women's Fellowship served a beautiful reception in Morris Parlors. It took two hours for everyone to come through the receiving line. Of course Mother and Dad, Frank and Lenora were in the line and little Mark stood right by my side the whole time.

After a quick change, Dr. Lemmon with Mother and Dad helped us escape the students who followed us after the reception. He got us to our car where I had hidden it behind a fraternity house so we could head south to Jefferson City where we spent our first night at the Capitol Hotel. Carol had eaten nothing at the reception so she sent me out at midnight for a sandwich before we got to bed for our first night together. The next day we went to a camp where we had vacationed earlier, then down the Natchez Trace through Mississippi to Natchez and Vicksburg. After a leisurely trip through Mississippi and Louisiana we got to New Orleans for services at the Lafayette Christian Church where Carnie was associate minister. Then across the Florida coast to Alabama and up to Birmingham where we stopped for a visit with Uncle Charley Washburn. Then to Chattanooga and finally to Russellville where we were greeted with a royal reception.

When we finally got back to Columbia we settled in with Carol's folks on Sexton Road for three months before moving to our first parsonage, the former home of Ella Evans on Locust Street. She had left her estate to the church, so they used it for us in its original condition. It was a nice home but needed much upkeep, so I spent some time painting the outside and papering the rooms. This would be our first home, and Cathie Ann was born while there on November 10, 1951 at the University hospital. It was a football Saturday and Dr. See had to be called back from the game when it was time for her to be delivered. Dr. Lemmon proudly announced the birth the next morning at church, saying, "why don't we name her Little Columbia?" I rushed back to the hospital after church to tell Carol that we had to name that child right away. We finally settled, naming her Catherine Ann for her two great-grandmothers. We were so proud of her that we took her to church the next Sunday and everywhere after that.

Carol had worked that first year as bookkeeper in the office of R. A. Miller, business manager of Christian College. This kept us involved with the school so that we were guests at dinners and other special occasions. Often I was asked to pray for academic functions. Although I was very busy with the church and CSC, I began taking courses at the University, working toward a Master's degree in history. I had classes in medieval history with Dr. Lewis Spitz, with whom I continued to keep in contact after leaving Columbia, and I have his definitive work in the medieval field and history of the Protestant Reformation. A course with a psychologist helped me to understand relationships in my counseling, as she had us write a biographical sketch. The colorful professor Jesse Wrench helped me greatly as he taught me the process of research. I don't remember much about his course on the Crusades, but I learned how to use and organize small card files, something which I often used in writing papers, sermon preparation and ultimately with the writing of several other works. I depended on this system long after my classes at the University as I began to read the letters of T. M. Allen in the Western Historical manuscripts at the University. This would grow into using further letters in the correspondence between Allen and John Allen Gano that would culminate in my thesis for the D.Min. degree—*Thomas Miller Allen, Pioneer Evangelist*. And still later I would use it in writing my part of *The Story of Logan County II* which I published in 2004. I didn't finish the degree, but I was able to use some of those courses for credit later in working for a master's degree in counseling at Northeast Missouri State College.

I was very much involved with Christian College and soon was asked to serve as advisor to the Vesper Board, helping students develop special religious programs. After a few years I was asked to teach the introductory religion course at the college, where Dr. Abram had been the teacher of all the religion courses. I thoroughly enjoyed the relationship with my students, but also had to serve as academic advisor for several students each semester, helping them determine courses which would be of help to them if they transferred to other schools after graduation. I had good friends among the faculty at Christian College. Bill Bedford was not only the music professor and later Dean of the college but the gifted organist at our church. Sidney Larson, head of the art department, became a close friend. We often had delightful evenings with Bill and Mary Alice Bedford and Sid and Georgeanne Larson. Both Dr. J. C. Miller, the president of the college, and R. A. Miller, the business manager, were leaders in our church, and they befriended us in many ways. I had a good relationship with the Bible College of Missouri, attending many of their worship services and meeting with the students as well as members of CSC. In working with their students I also became good friends of the Stephens College leadership as well as the administration and faculty of the University.

My fraternity, Phi Kappa Psi, had a chapter in Columbia, Missouri - Alpha. I visited them often in my early days and they soon asked me to serve as their chapter advisor, which I did for several years. This mainly involved attending their special activities and dances. Carol and I enjoyed this after we were married.

We enjoyed the life of the three campuses. We heard many lectures, outstanding musical programs, and well known speakers who came to the colleges. I especially remember hearing Eleanor Roosevelt when she spoke at Stephens College. The St. Louis Symphony often played at the University as did other outstanding musical groups. We attended most basketball and football games. This was the heyday of Missouri football under Coach Don Faurot. Oklahoma almost always beat Missouri in those days. But Missouri beat SMU in its better days, Vanderbilt, and many fine teams. We belonged to the Stephens College Country Club, which was a wonderful place for families, with swimming and picnic facilities. I played golf there many years. Columbia is close to the Lake of the Ozarks, which provided many opportunities for family outings as well as the camps which we used at CSC retreats. One special week we enjoyed at the Lake when we rented a large cabin that we shared with the Bedfords and Larsons. One day when the parents told the kids to behave, Nancy Larson said, "I'm being-have." And we never let her forget it.

Living in the same community as Carol's parents was a real asset. I had spent lots of time at their home and later we were often there for Sunday dinners. Frank said he thought when Carol and I were married, he wouldn't have to continue to feed me. But almost every Sunday after church we had Lenora's delightful dinners as well as many other special occasions. They were great in taking care of Cathie, and of course in later years all three girls. It was at this time that Lenora began making dresses for Cathie as she continued to do for all three girls.

Some time after beginning to make the Locust Street house a real home, we acquired a small kitten which soon became a very large Puddy Cat. He was a favorite in the neighborhood and very important in our lives as our first pet. After Cathie was born and Carol still in the hospital, Puddy Cat got caught high up in a tree outside our home I had a most difficult time rescuing him, for I knew Carol would be very upset if anything had happened to our cat. Fortunately, cat and baby took to each other and Cathie was well guarded by our pet. Cathie's first birthday was a real delight. She was mature enough by this time that she took full advantage of the occasion. I remember her sitting by our big square record player and playing the small children's records.

The next summer we made plans to attend our national student conference in Estes Park, Colorado. Cathie was a year and a half old and we planned to take her with us. We also took one of the leaders of the Christian Student Congregation,

Marjorie Dysart. One of the families in our church, the Alex Bradfords, took an especial interest in us and they insisted that we must come by to see them in Colorado Springs where they would be staying at the Colorado Springs Hotel The Bradfords had given us a fine set of luggage for the trip and had made arrangements for us to stay at a motel in Colorado Springs. They had us for dinner at the hotel and made plans for us to drive to the top of Pike's Peak while we were there. It so happened that Bob Simpich, who had been an active leader and president of CSC was spending the summer there and drove the limousine that took us to the top of the Peak.

It was not long before we began to think of another child. Carol Lee was also born in the University hospital on July 20. 1954. It was a terribly hot night, before the time of air conditioning in many homes. Waiting to go to the hospital Carol and I went to a movie the night she was expecting just to stay cool. Frank and Lenora had Cathie at home while we waited. It was another exciting time when Carol Lee arrived, receiving her mother's and grandmother's names. Dad said he was happy she had the name of a Confederate general, Lee. The only thing better might have been to name her Carol Lee Beauregard. From that big nickname came the use of Little Beauregard, which soon was shortened to Little Beaure, and eventually to Little Bo, which has clung to her through the years.

After we began to have a family, it became obvious that the parsonage on Locust Street was too small. After some negotiation, the leaders of the church began to look for a more adequate home for the associate minister. This was a little difficult because Dr. Lemmon owned his own home and the church was not accustomed to providing a parsonage. But the time came when they purchased a house on Garth Avenue which was still being constructed. When we moved in, the yard had not been landscaped and was a source of dust and sometimes mud. But the inconvenience was worth while, for soon we were settled into a most comfortable home with built-in garage, a large screened-in porch across the back, and a very pleasant neighborhood. We were just across the street from the Grant elementary school, which would be most attractive for Cathie as she was growing to school age.

Garth Avenue was a fortunate place for us at that time. Next door to us was a family with a girl of Cathie's age, Mary Fields, and they played well together. Just a block south of us were Tom and Mildred Shrout and their children, Martha and Tommy. Carol and Mildred became close friends, and our kids made them a second home so close at hand. Carol Lee loved butter and sugar on a slice of bread and when she had licked it clean, she often took the bread back to Mildred for a second serving. The couple next door to the north of us were older but very good neighbors. We remember our days on Garth Avenue with great pleasure, but we regret that a few years after we moved to Kirksville this block was eliminated to make room for the expansion of the public library on the corner of Main and Garth Streets.

After we went to Columbia, Bradley and Margaret had progressed with their lives in Western Kentucky and then in Nashville. Margaret graduated from

Olmstead High School as she had promised her folks she would. Then they moved to Murray where Brad studied at Murray State University. When he graduated in June of 1946, Alben Barclay gave the commencement address. Jack Russell was running the Disciple house in Murray for young men preparing for the ministry. Jack encouraged him to begin preaching and found opportunities in nearby churches. Soon Bradley was asked to serve the church at Mt. Hermon, near the Ohio River. He took his work seriously, working hard on his sermons, with support from Dad. He would occasionally go to the church in Russellville while he was preaching at Mt. Hermon to practice his sermons.

After Bradley received his A.B. from Murray, having prepared to teach, he and Margaret moved to Nashville, where he entered the Divinity School at Vanderbilt. He had a great experience at Vanderbilt where he found a fellow student in Herman Norton, who later became an outstanding professor in the Divinity School and director of the Vanderbilt Disciples House. Another of his fellow students was Henry Campbell, who became a close friend. Bradley and Margaret lived in the Disciples House at 2005 Grand Avenue, where I had lived while in the Divinity School. Bradley applied himself to his studies and did quite well. Margaret worked at Loveman's Department store in Nashville and also did some work at the office of the Divinity School. Bradley accepted calls as pastor of the Berea, Auburn and Daysville Christian Churches in Logan County, Kentucky, which meant they came to Russellville on the weekends. While at Auburn Bradley held a revival, with his father doing the preaching. They worked hard visiting prospective members. He did an outstanding job serving the Berea church. I was delighted to find an excellent tribute to his work in a history of the Berea church which I found recently in our Logan County library. I found this quote:

"In 1947 Berea called a very young man, the son of a former pastor—Bradley Coffman. Bradley began to wake up the church to greater possibilities of a wider field of usefulness. Through his influence the Auburn, Daysville and Berea churches decided to work together with Bradley as pastor of all three. He organized the Berea Christian Youth Fellowship, with Mr. and Mrs. Winfred Violett as sponsors. "The blessings this C.Y.F. has brought to the church and the young people cannot be measured," wrote the church historian. Bradley also spurred the church to greater missionary effort. Although his leadership was cut short by a fatal illness, the seeds he planted in the hearts and minds of the Berea people have grown and flowered."

During his second year in seminary, Bradley's health began to deteriorate. The nephritis which would eventually cause his death was progressing. When Carol and I were married on June 5, 1949, he was not able to come to Columbia to be the Best Man for our wedding. Realizing that his future was uncertain he and Margaret talked Grandmother Coffman into letting them make a small apartment in the back rooms of her home in Russellville. They installed a small bathroom and a wall kitchen and breakfast unit in the east room and used the west room for their living and bedroom. It was very comfortable and quite attractive, with

Margaret's decorative touches. Bradley continued to serve his churches until his health became serious in the spring of 1950. In the meantime, Margaret became pregnant, and Bradley was looking forward to the coming of a son. He would not live to see the birth of little Bradley the next fall.

Bradley was becoming so seriously ill that Mother called me one Sunday morning saying that we should try to come home immediately, for she was not sure he could live much longer. We left right after church that morning and drove as rapidly as possible. But the weather was so bad that we had to spend the night in Carbondale, Illinois. When we got home about noon the next day, it was obvious that Bradley needed to be taken to the hospital, so we left very soon for Nashville. We followed Mother and Dad and we stayed most of that week in Nashville at Vanderbilt Hospital with them while the doctors were doing everything possible to improve Bradley's condition. The doctors were surprised that Bradley had been so careful about avoiding salt in his diet that there was virtually no salt in his system when he arrived at the hospital. The night we arrived we parked our beautiful new Mercury automobile in the parking lot of the hospital. When we came out about one o'clock it had been stolen. We reported it immediately, and sometime the next morning they called to say they had found it abandoned with its wheels missing somewhere near Bordeaux, a suburb of Nashville. They had pulled out the back seat in order to take out the spare tire and in the process they trampled a lot of good food we had brought from Russellville. A beautiful cake was crushed in the ground. It did not take us long to get the loss adjusted and our new car restored to its original condition. Carol and I returned to Columbia the next weekend and Bradley was sent home about that time. But his condition continued to deteriorate and so we returned to Russellville. One morning, his breath began to leave him. He had fought a long, hard fight, but at the age of twenty-five his beautiful life came to a close. Mother and Dad had lost the second of their three children.

As was our custom, the casket stayed in our living room to receive visitors. Margaret wanted to stay with Bradley that first night so Carol and I slept in the living room with her. The funeral was at the First Christian Church in Russellville, with the pastor, presiding. Dean John Keith Benton of the Divinity School participated and several members of the faculty came for the service. Dr. C. E. Lemmon, my senior pastor, had a prayer. Elders of Bradley's three churches participated, and many of their members were there. The outpouring of flowers was so great that the florists held back many of the orders until they could be used Sunday after Sunday at the churches. Herman Norton and Henry Campbell were among the pallbearers. Within a year Henry would marry Margaret and begin a long life in a very close relationship with all our family. When little Bradley was born, Henry became his earthly father. After he was growing up Bradley used to say that Henry was his father here and his other father was in heaven. This was the beginning of a long and dedicated relationship, with Henry leaving a loving example for Bradley, which was a moving influence on his life. Young Bradley didn't become a minister, but he has been a dedicated churchman and an attorney exhibiting great concern for people in his work.

I have often reflected on the strange development of our lives as children. My sister and brother were both pictures of health until their untoward illnesses. Sister was very athletic, a beautiful swimmer and involved in a very busy life until at the age of sixteen she developed what proved to be leukemia, for which there was then no known cure and very little treatment. Bradley was a strong, well-built young man, extremely talented physically. He was captain of his football team, played basketball, swam with great strength, played outstanding golf, and until his nephritis made itself felt, was a fine physical specimen. He enlisted in the Army with his friend Brents Thurmond. They were sent to Ft. Thomas, but after two weeks Bradley was sent home. The doctors had discovered his kidney problem that proved to be nephritis. He was then eighteen, but he fought valiantly for seven years. He had graduated from Murray, completed two years of Divinity School, and begun an amazing ministry. When he died at the age of twenty-five he left a beautiful, well-lived life.

On the other hand, I was the least physically fit of the three of us. I had pneumonia two or three times in my earliest years. I was so small and slow developing that some of my family thought I would not live to be grown. But somehow I survived, was small and underweight for years, had serious asthma and all the usual childhood illnesses. I have had four-by-pass surgery and several other surgeries, but I am still reasonably healthy. Several weeks ago Dr. Hayden gave me a thorough physical. He could find nothing wrong with me. In fact, he said that if he were in as good condition as I am when he is my age, he would consider himself very fortunate. So now in my old age, being quite active and alert, I think it is amazing that I am the only one of three children to survive. Mother told me that God had great plans for my life. I don't know why she thought so, but I do know that she and Dad were very pleased with my ministry. Dad told me once that my sermons were excellent, better even than Dr. Lemmon's. He had heard us both many times. I know that was a father's pride, but I appreciated it. I hope that my life has been worthwhile and I may have lived up to the expectations that Mother had for me.

First Christian Church, Columbia, Missouri;

Outside my office at FCC Columbia

CSC Group

Lenora and Frank Alexander – Carol's Parents

Carol Jean and Ed Just Dating;

Carol Jean and Ed Off to a Dance

Our Wedding Day

Our Wedding Party

Going Away Outfits

Ed with Young Cathie and Carol Lee

5

Kirksville, Missouri

During my years as campus minister I visited several churches where we had campus organizations. One of these was Kirksville, Missouri, the home of Northeast Missouri State Teachers College. When our state student convention was in Kirksville I became acquainted with several members of the First Christian Church. And we had had numerous students from Kirksville in CSC in Columbia. This combination must have led the Kirksville church in asking me to become their pastor. After twelve years as a campus minister I had rather assumed that this might be my future. But since Kirksville was a campus church I considered it seriously. Eldon Drennan had been president of CSC and his father, Ollin Drennan, was chairman of the pulpit committee. After long consideration, Carol and I decided that this might be a worthwhile ministry for us. We made a visit to the Kirksville church and were impressed with the vitality of the congregation and the new Educational Building adjacent to the old church.

When we accepted the call to Kirksville we were treated royally. They had a parsonage at 416 S.Halliburton Street in which my predecessor, Romans Smith, had lived a short time. The house needed redecoration and they gave us a free hand to make all the decisions about papering and painting of every room. This was to be our home for nine happy years. There were many children in the neighborhood and our girls thoroughly enjoyed the opportunity to have young friends. Whenever they went outside there were always several children around for a good time. Ann Bondurant lived across the street, Alan, Charlie and Mary Harrington, lived a block behind our house. Punk and Sarah Lehr were wonderful neighbors next door. The Walter Beards first lived across the street and then the Huenemans. Just a block down the street was Greenwood School where all our girls had an excellent start. The principal, Leslie White, lived between us and the school. He took an especial interest in our girls and gave them great support. This excellent neighborhood made it difficult for us to leave after those most pleasant years in Kirksville.

My ministry in Kirksville was quite different from my twelve years in Columbia. I was no longer a campus minister, dealing weekly with hundreds of college students who changed with each semester. Now I was the senior pastor of a well functioning congregation, with the weekly routine of sermons, administration, visitation and hospital calling, counseling, and community groups. Our sanctuary was old-fashioned with a large stained glass window at the rear, single pulpit, fairly good organ and choir loft, baptistry in the floor of the chancel behind the pulpit, and an unfinished basement where the furnace and hot water heater were located. There were no separate faucets for hot and cold water so that the baptistry had to be filled first and then hot water added. This once caused a problem when the water was too hot and we had to wait for some time for it to be cool enough to use. It was obvious that the sanctuary needed to be rebuilt and this was being planned before I left. Soon plans were made to remove the old building and build a fine new sanctuary.

Across the driveway was the new Educational Building with secretary's office, my office with an outside entrance, then the library which was used for many committee meetings, then a large parlor which was used for Board and group meetings as well as many receptions. Neva Miller was my secretary all the years we were there. Across the hall was a Sunday School office, nursery, and graded classrooms. On the lower level were a well equipped kitchen and a social hall large enough to serve up to as many as 200 for meals but could be divided with folding doors into three large adult classrooms. It was quite functional and was used by many groups in the community as well as for our regular programs. Behind the sanctuary was a large old home on a lot which the church later bought in order to have room for a new sanctuary. The house included several apartments and was used for several years as a parsonage for the Associate Minister.

The parsonage at 416 S. Halliburton was large and commodious. When we arrived, we were told that it needed redecorating and we were to do it ourselves. We were to decide on paper and paint for every room there. It had an entryway and large living room, dining room and kitchen. There was a family room and utility room on the side. Upstairs were four large bedrooms to which we piped music on our record player. The girls grew up listening to many of our great musicals which they still remember well. In front was a full length porch which we enjoyed greatly until in later years it was replaced with a small entrance stoop, to the dismay of our girls.

As the girls were growing up, we often had devotionals around a coffee table in the living room. They would set up a worship center and take part in the scripture and prayers. We always had blessings before meals. One day we were singing the Johnny Appleseed song: "Oh the Lord's been good to me, and so I thank the Lord for giving me the things I need, the sun, the rain, and the apple seed, the Lord's been good to me." Young Alan Harrington was outside our window and he called up, "Sing it again." I often read stories for the girls before bedtime. Over the course of the years we read almost all of the Tom Sawyer and Huckleberry Finn books.

We had fine neighbors. Sarah and Punk Lehr helped us in many ways. She was great with the girls, inviting them over for breakfast on many occasions. Punk spent many hours watering his beautiful flowers and often invited me to share his big color TV. I saw the first Super Bowl game with him the last month I was there. Across the street were Bill and Ruth Bondurant, whose daughter Ann was a good friend of our girls and son David. There were many children in our neighborhood who played together beautifully. Any time they came out there might be ten or twelve having a great time. Many of them decided to organize a Fourth of July parade. Cathie and Carol Lee took the lead. They made posters and went to the radio station to advertise it. They had the fire engine to lead the parade and a police car for protection. Many children marched or rode bicycles or trikes, some pulling smaller ones in wagons. Dogs and other animals joined in the fun. This became a very successful annual affair as long as we lived in Kirksville. Another family lived not from us for a time on Halliburton, Dr. and Mrs. Taylor Lindsey. He taught Spanish at the college. Their daughter Robin was a good friend of Cathie. She had a sister Joanne who was an artist. who painted a nice portrait of Connie at age six which we have on the wall of our upstairs bedroom in Russellville.

My life was soon extremely busy with all the committees and age-level groups. Of course I had many funerals and weddings, counseling sessions, and requests to speak to various organizations. Soon my relationship with Dr. Walter Ryle, President of Kirksville State Teachers College (soon to be Northeast Missouri State University) and faculty members meant that I was often asked to have the Invocation for college functions and to preach baccalaureate and commencement services on occasion. Within a short time I was serving on the Board of the Community Nursing Homes, the Missouri Mental Health Association, the Red Cross blood program, the Boy Scout Council, and many other organizations. I was appointed to the Board of the Missouri School of Religion, which meant monthly trips to Columbia. For the Christian Church in Missouri I was a member of the regional board and chairman of the student work program. The Third District of the Christian Church in Missouri required many meetings of the ministers in the area and work on various committees. Each year I was in Kirksville I was a member of the faculty of the CYF Conference held on the campus of Culver-Stockton College in Canton. Every year we attended the International Convention of the Christian Church, which was held in different parts of the country. This often provided opportunity to take our family on nice trips.

The parsonage on Halliburton was just a block from Greenwood School, which the girls enjoyed greatly. The principal was Leslie White. He was especially nice to us, helping the girls in many ways. When they were growing up we often wanted to take them with us to conventions. Mr. White would say sure, take them, the experience would be more important than the few days they might miss at school. Mr. White's wife, Lanear, was a fine teacher. She was working on a degree in the summers at the University of Vermont, and we visited them once when there on a trip. The girls had good teachers at Greenwood School, and there were many interesting activities in the curriculum. Cathie and Carol Lee participated in many special day programs and dance groups. Connie also started to school there and it was especially hard for her to change schools when we moved.

My involvement in the national student work program meant regular conferences in which we could involve our entire family. The Fellowship of Campus Ministry Conference in August of 1959 was at Estes Park, Colorado. We thoroughly enjoyed the national Y facilities and sharing with the families of our fellow campus ministers. Cathie was eight years old and very precocious. I remember a fall which she had from a high slide when she got gravel in her lip which stayed with her for years. We enjoyed lots of activities, including a small railroad for the children which they remember riding in later years there at Estes. The campus ministry conference was followed by the national Disciples Student Fellowship Conference that year, when many students came from our campus to Denver, so we enjoyed that part of the country. Similar conferences followed through the years we were in Kirksville.

Our church was only two blocks from the courthouse and the center of town. We had several families in the church in business on the square so I spent many hours visiting the Anderson jewelry company, John Harrington's jewelry store, Edna Campbell's delightful book store and the Gardner-Collier jewelry store. I also found a good friend in Bamburg men's clothing store.

We had some very fine members of our church who became long-time friends. Charles and Gertrude Krueger were especially supportive. Charles was the manager of the Chamber of Commerce and a strong leader in the community. He encouraged me to take an active part in community affairs. He and Gertrude were fine leaders of the congregation and took us under their wing, often inviting us to their home and entertaining the girls. They had two fine sons, Fred and Charles.

Ruby and Mary Green and their daughter Rosemary befriended us in many ways. They invited an exchange student from New Zealand to spend a year in their home. She and Rosemary became close friends and they later visited each other in their homes.

Dr. and Mrs. Chester Atteberry (Louella) had a cottage on Spring Lake to which they often invited us. Their children were active in the youth program of our church. Dr. Atteberry was the son-in-law of Dr. Hardy, both of whom were fine osteopathic physicians and surgeons. Soon after we went to Kirksville I had difficulty with my nose. After some treatment, Dr. Atteberry operated, cutting out part of the septum and opening up the sinuses. I was in the Kirksville Osteopathic Hospital five days and received good manipulations from Dr. Bill Kelly, another good friend and member of our congregation. He and Margaret were wonderful supporters of our ministry through the years.

Harold Epperson was our choir director and he and Lathella became close friends. We spent many hours in their home. He owned a music store on the square and through him we were able to secure instruments for our girls. Long after we left Kirksville he sold us a cello at a greatly reduced price for Connie, which she played through Junior High School. We still saw Lathella often, until her passing, and her daughter Beth, and son Joe. Edna Campbell was another good member of our church who owned a fine bookstore on the square downtown. She took great delight in making new books available to her pastor, often before publication time. She was especially nice to the girls and gave them many nice gifts.

John and Louise Harrington were close friends who lived a block behind the parsonage, and owned a jewelry store on the square. Their son Alan was just a year older than Connie, whom he adored. He stood by her crib when she was a baby and through the years became a long time friend. Their daughter Mary was a fine leader in our youth program who later married Bob Flanagan, who entered the ministry while I was there. The Beard family were long-time supporters and friends, continuing long after we left. Walter and Gladys were the older parents. Walter owned a fine paint store on the square. Three generations of Beards were wonderful leaders in the church and continue to this day.

The Ollin Drennans were a fine family in the church He had suggested me to the pulpit committee when they were looking for a pastor. Their son Eldon had been President of CSC. He was a graduate of the School of Journalism at the University of Missouri. Later he studied for the ministry at Drake University and succeeded me as director of the Christian Student Congregation. His brother was also active in the Kirksville church. Stan and Doris Bohon and their children Rick, Connie and Libby became our life-long friends whom we still visit in Florida and Kirksville. Dr. Bohon took care of our girls' teeth. John and Sue Winn lived on the corner of the block of the church. John was an insurance salesman who helped me in many ways. Sue was a music teacher who gave our girls piano lessons. They had two daughters who were our girls age. We spent many hours together.

My relationship with Charles Krueger, who was executive of the Chamber of Commerce, led me to spend much time in visiting the city council and other official groups. One of the most satisfying was my relationship with Wayne Bell, the city school superintendent. He came to me one day with an interest in a new program that the government was just instituting called Head Start. He hoped we could be one of the first communities to begin such a program. Since it badly needed facilities, I suggested that the Christian Church might be willing to use its building during weekdays for such a program for pre-school children, especially from low-income families. Our church gave its approval and in 1964 we started one of the first Head Start programs, which was one of the first in the nation. I worked closely with the school and helped to bring children who had no transportation. One of these was Billy, whose little dog was his only friend. I brought Billy to school many mornings and took him to shop for things he needed. I look back on this Head Start program as one of the most creative things I did during my years in Kirksville.

As pastor of the Christian Church, I worked closely with other churches in the community. I served as President of the Ministerial Association and led in cooperative community programs. The pastor of the Methodist Church across the street was a good friend and co-worker and we had close relationships with the Presbyterian Church and the First Baptist Church. Our church was quite open to groups that wanted to use our building for special functions. We had many outside groups which met there. and other churches sometimes used our sanctuary or baptistry for weddings and other affairs. Doc Mason was organizing a new Church of Christ congregation. He was much more liberal than the other Church of Christ groups. I was able to offer him the use of our baptistry for his baptismal services and our sanctuary for weddings and other programs. Dr. Dale Jorgenson came to Kirksville to teach at the college. He was a minister and I was able to help him get started with nearby churches. The family continues to be active in our congregation.

We had a good relationship with Doris Akers, who wrote the hymn "There's a Sweet, Sweet Spirit In This Place", found in our Disciple Hymnal. Doris was the daughter of a fine family in Kirksville. She was living in Los Angeles but often came home. When she did, the whole family would come to our church and Doris would sing the hymn she had written and others for us. A beautiful memory when we sing it in our church today.

During our Kirksville years we spent lots of time camping. As the girls grew up, we soon learned that we could camp across the country for a week for much less than one or two days staying in motels. The girls simply grew up in camp settings and through the years have continued their love of camping. Our first tent when Cathie was a baby was a small pup tent which I had used as a Scoutmaster. Our first outings were almost disasters, for we had no idea of cooking utensils or other equipment for outdoor living. We soon graduated to a one room umbrella tent large enough for our sleeping bags on the floor. We began to acquire light-weight cooking utensils, a large Coleman lantern, and eventually a gas cook stove. Early in my Kirksville years I found the design for a wood camp cabinet designed to hold our cooking utensils, food and other equipment. I built it so that it fit into the rear of the station wagon which had been become a staple for our camp life. It served us well and now has a place of honor in our attic. The time came when we moved from the umbrella tent to a three-room tent large enough for all of our growing family. Eventually, we brought a camp trailer with four bunk beds and a small kitchen unit with running water which served us well until long after we moved to Madisonville.

The Thousand Hills State Park was seven miles west of town. It was in its early years when we went there and we grew up with it. There were excellent fishing, boating and picnic areas. We spent many hours at the park during those years. The campground was well equipped and we camped there often, finding many friends who shared our love of outdoor life. We often would pitch our tent for several days at a time, the whole family camping while I went in to town each day. Eventually, a dining room was built and we often went to the park for meals. There were plans being made for cabins, but they were never built while we were there. With fellow campers we became involved in the National Campers and Hikers Association and joined in its activities. One year we went to the national NCHA camp event in Bowling Green, Kentucky. Several thousand campers were there at Beech Bend Park, on the Barren River, which had an excellent swimming pool. There was a great parade of campers in downtown Bowling Green while we were there. Of course, we have known Beech Bend through the years, and we manage to spend some time there on family outings.

During those years we went to all our church conventions. These included: St. Louis in 1958, Denver in 1959, Louisville in 1960, and Kansas City in 1961. The next year we went by train to the International Convention at Los Angeles. Mother and Dad went with us and we boarded the Santa Fe train at La Plata, Missouri just south of Kirksville for an overnight trip to LA. It was quite an adventure, with seven of us and all our baggage which we would count whenever we boarded. We slept in our seats, and took our food with us. It was too expensive for the diner. We enjoyed all the sites in LA: Disney World, Knott's Berry Farm, etc. I preached on the Sunday of the convention at the church of my friend Sam McClain in Riverside, Ca. The last night of the convention we went to see the Ringling Brothers, Barnum and Bailey Circus. We took the Southern Pacific to San Francisco overnight. We rented a car and spent the day seeing the city by trolley and the Muir Woods up north. We returned home by a different route, taking two days before we reached Kansas City. We went to church there on Sunday morning, but no one greeted us except a couple from Kirksville.

In 1963 the convention was in Miami Beach and we went by train, joining several other ministers. We enjoyed the pleasant weather and playing in the surf in the afternoons. By 1963 Dr. Lemmon had died, so Carol and I took Mrs. Lemmon with us to the World Convention at San Juan, Puerto Rico. We flew home through Jamaica where we spent some time with our missionaries from Kirksville, Dewayne and LaVerne Wellborn. Carol and I drove to the 1964 convention in Detroit. The 1966 convention was in Dallas where we heard Dr. Martin Luther King speak. Carol and I sent home a chair for Mother and Dad for their wedding anniversary.

Another Kirksville attraction was Spring Lake, a development where many families owned summer homes. We were often invited to their cottages for picnics and fishing. One of the most used was the home of Dr. and Mrs. Atteberry, who often invited our youth groups for outings. The Beard family and others also had nice homes which they shared with us.

Kirksville was the home of osteopathy and we were surrounded by the profession. Very important in the life of the community was the Kirksville College of Osteopathy and Surgery, where many of the doctors in our church practiced. We were not too familiar with osteopathy when we went there, but it became very important in our lives. We soon learned that D.O.'s have essentially the same training as M.D.'s but with an added feature of osteopathic manipulation which is very attractive. They were sometimes referred to as "rubbing doctors" because of the way they treated the muscles and nerves. We had a large number of D.O.s in our congregation, but no M.D.s. There were two osteopathic hospitals in Kirksville, Laughlin and Kirksville Osteopathic, and one M.D. .hospital, Grimm-Smith. They were all good, and I spent many hours calling on many of their patients.

Carol had never had a child without Dr. See in Columbia, so she had some reservation about her upcoming pregnancy. But when Constance Sue, named in honor of Constance Lemmon was delivered December 3, 1958, with no difficulty, Carol said she could not have had any better care anywhere. The morning Connie was born I called Frank and Lenora to tell them of their new granddaughter, saying she was "ugly as sin", which she was, but as soon as she was cleaned up she was a beautiful little girl. However, Lenora never forgave me.

One time Cathie was in the hospital at KOH for a tonsillectomy and while she was there Connie had an ear infection which sent her to the hospital, so they were both there at the same time receiving especially good care. We soon came to love and appreciate these "rubbing doctors."

Soon after we went to Kirksville I was asked to teach religion courses for the Missouri School of Religion at Northeast Missouri State. This was arranged with the college so that students could take the courses for credit. I taught several different courses during the time I was there. In the process I became very close to the administration of the college. The President, Dr. Walter Ryle, and I became good friends. He often asked me to participate in college programs, having the invocation or in other ways being involved. He even had me deliver the baccalaureate address one year before commencement.

I also began to take classes at the college and soon was working on a degree in guidance in the College of Education. I developed a close relationship with Dr Jack Reiske who taught several of my courses. He arranged for me to take a test that would allow me to proceed in the educational program without having to take some of the preliminary courses. Before we moved to Madisonville I had taken all but four hours needed for the Master's degree. The next summer I took two courses at the University of Evansville, completed the necessary requirements, and in 1967 I received the MA degree in Guidance at what is now Truman University.

Cathie was a good student at Greenwood School, just a block from our home on South Halliburton. She was soon reading everything she could get her hands on and playing the piano. Carol Lee at six was in the first grade, taking baton lessons. The next summer we went to Florida for a week's vacation with Mother and Dad. The next year Bo in the second grade at Greenwood School was a Brownie Scout. Cathie in the fourth grade was studying Spanish and playing the piano. Their grandmother, Lenora, was in a bad accident and was hospitalized in Macon for some time and then at home for several weeks.

The next year, 1962, the girls, with several of their friends in the neighborhood, started their famous Fourth of July Parade. They made posters and went to the radio station to promote it. They had police to lead the parade and a fire engine at the rear. This attracted many viewers and became an annual affair until we left Kirksville.

The next year Connie Sue was in the Community Nursery School sponsored by the Episcopal Church, in which Carol would later work. The vicar of the church was Reverend Harry Maurer. Connie didn't understand that he was not married., When we explained to her that he was a bachelor, she said "he's a smart-thinking bachelor." Carol Lee in the fourth grade was a Girl Scout and Cathie added violin lessons to piano and Scouting. In 1964 Connie finished Nursery School and was soon a six year old kindergartner at Greenwood School. Carol Lee was in the elementary school chorus, piano and Girl Scouts along with archery and baton at the Family Y. Cathie completed the sixth grade with a beautiful class program and in the fall she was a Junior High School student, playing the flute in the band, chorus, Pep Club, Scouts, plus baton and square dancing at the Y. Our whole family with Mother and Dad enjoyed the World's Fair in New York. In August we spent a week at the Philmont Scout Ranch in New Mexico as I participated in a Protestant Relations Workshop. This was a great experience with separate activities for Carol and each of the girls. Then Carol and I attended the International Convention of the Christian Church in Detroit.

One winter I went to New York and Washington for the United Nations Seminar which was sponsored by our denomination. I took a bus to St. Louis but found my plane flight had been cancelled because of bad weather. As a result I had to take a later flight which landed several times in bad storms. We spent three days in New York at the UN buildings, involved in training and attending one session of the Security Council. We went to Washington for the last two days of the Seminar, attending sessions of Congress and spending an evening at the National City Christian Church, where the organist was a fine young man from Jefferson City, Missouri, whom I had had in summer conference earlier. Two yeas later Carol took three young people from our CYF group which she sponsored to the United Nations Seminar. And still later Cathie would go to the Seminar by herself.

One fall Dad was selected as the Guest of Honor at the Logan County Tobacco Festival. We all went to Russellville for the great occasion. There were several special events during the week, including a fine banquet in tribute to the Guest of Honor. Dad was the Grand Marshall of the Parade on Saturday. He and Mother led the parade and then sat in the viewer's stand as all the floats and bands passed. That afternoon Russellville was playing in the festival football game at Rhea Stadium and Dad was very much involved. As had become the custom, the cheer leaders had him come down to lead cheers at halftime.

On the occasion of my parents' 50th wedding anniversary in the fall of 1966, someone brought a little dog to the door as a gift to Dad and Mother from Otis Cooper. As they weren't really equipped to have a dog, I volunteered to give the dog a home. Dad said we couldn't have a dog because I was allergic to them. But I realized it was a Chihuahua and knew that they were not supposed to be problems for asthma. So I asked Dad to accept the gift. Connie immediately named him Snoopy, and she was waiting eagerly at the corner of Normal and Halliburton Streets as I drove home with him. Snoopy was small and loving and soon was the center of our household. We took him with us when we moved to Madisonville a short time later and he lived several years in the new home on Park Avenue.

Our years in Kirksville were most satisfying. I enjoyed my ministry and the time I spent in teaching at the college and taking classes which eventually led to a Master's degree. The girls had many happy experiences growing up and left with a large number of good friends. Carol spent several years helping with the preschool program at the Episcopal Church, which was a prelude to the forming of the pre-school program which was later so successful after we went to Madisonville. It was not easy to make the decision to leave Kirksville after nine years to begin the next major phase of our lives in Madisonville.

First Christian Church, Kirksville, Missouri

Cathie and Carol Lee at Easter

Connie Sue Arrives

The Family Welcomes Connie Sue

Decorating the Girl's Christmas Tree

Decorating the Family Christmas Tree

Family Devotional
During Advent

Philmont, New Mexico

Front Porch in Kirksville

Graduation from Northeast Missouri State

6

Madisonville, Kentucky

James and Jessie Simmons and Marlon and Dixie Rakestraw had come to visit us in Kirksville when the Madisonville church was looking for a new minister. They spent a memorable weekend when Carol served them a delicious meal. We then went to Madisonville to talk with the full committee. Edwin and Lanna McGary had us for dinner in their home. Edwin took me to help sell Kiwanis peanuts during the Thanksgiving parade. And thus began a long friendship which continued through the years. The Madisonville church asked us to come as their pastor, an invitation we gladly accepted. Lanna was later accepted by the West area as a lay minister and has preached often in recent years. At this writing Edwin is in the Alzheimer hospital just north of Madisonville. The Rakestraws and their daughter Lista were good friends and supporters all the years we were there, but are all now deceased. James and Jessie were our close friends through the years. He had grown up in Russellville and had a fond appreciation for both of my folks and me. Jessie was a fine teacher. All of our girls had her for home economics classes and loved her dearly. She died early in 2010 and James preceded her by several years.

Our first days in Madisonville marked the first of twenty very happy years there. Here all three girls graduated from high school and college and received Master's degrees before beginning a great variety of business lives. And here Carol started the Nursery School that would grow from six students to over a hundred in the last years before we retired in 1987. Madisonville became the prime years of our lives.

We left Kirksville on a cold snowy afternoon for the long drive to Madisonville. Frank and Lenora joined us as we were driving both the Dodge station wagon and the Vauxhall, pulling the camper. Connie got sick which delayed us some time, so it was close to midnight before we arrived at our new home on Friday. The van with our furniture was late so we had to wait one day to unload. I had to go to Mammoth Cave on Saturday for a church meeting, so Carol was left to unload and place our furniture with the help of both sets of grandparents. By Sunday morning, though, we were ready for my first sermon as pastor of the First Christian Church of Madisonville. We were received warmly, and then Sunday evening we invited several who had participated in our first service for dinner at home. To the amazement of everyone, Carol, with the help of the grandparents served a delicious meal.

We hit the ground running. I had already made arrangements for several things to be done by the time we got there. We had planned for a Pastor's Class on Church Membership and it started our first week. We soon were involved in pre-Easter evangelism and had good response. Eighteen of the young people in the Pastor's Class united with the church and were baptized on Palm Sunday and Easter. I preached for several nights of services before Easter. Soon we had twenty-two of our members attending the Kentucky State Convention in Owensboro.

We had an excellent Sunday School. Ben Ashmore was the superintendent and four men were the secretaries, distributing literature to the classrooms and keeping the records. The Ashmore family became good friends through the years. I had the wedding of their daughter, Ginny; Jim introduced us to Emmaus; and Virginia was our choir director when we were in the new building later.

During Christian Family Week we honored couples who had been married fifty-years or more and dedicated young children. Twenty-one of our young people were graduating from high school and Carol had them for open house at the parsonage. Carol was very soon involved in many activities and that summer directed our Vacation Church School.

Our new parsonage was wonderful. It had been built from a floor plan they had found in a magazine and was only a year old. The former pastor's family had only lived there six months before they moved to Richmond, Kentucky where Charles Blakemore had been called as pastor of the First Christian Church. At 560 Park Avenue, the house had a large sloping lot about a mile from the church. To the north was the home of Mrs. Lizzie Nisbet, a true saint and great neighbor. Past her was the home of Clyde and Lorena Ruby, on a large wooded lot. To the south were Roy and Betty Stoltz, who became our long time neighbors. Just below us was the land of the city park with a small lake. While we were there it was developed into a fine golf course where I often played.

There were no small children in the neighborhood, which we found to be a problem for Connie. But we soon found a good friend for her, Ben Holloway, who lived a few blocks away and soon came to visit often. We were most fortunate in finding that her second grade teacher at Hall Street Elementary School was Sissy Finley, a member of our church. Sissy took an especial interest in her and helped her greatly to adjust to the move that had been so difficult for her. We had no great problems of adjustment for Cathie and Carol Lee. Cathie caught on quickly as a freshman at the Madisonville High School, though she was not accepted as quickly as we would have liked. Carol Lee fit in soon at the eighth grade in the Junior High School. In a short time she had many good friends.

Life was soon very busy for us. But we had some problems in getting used to the more segregated life style than we had known in Kirksville. This was the beginning of the civil rights revolution with many social adjustments. It caused us some difficulties since I was too liberal for many people. My sermons sometimes aroused displeasure from those who were less tolerant of my views. And occasionally there would be criticism of the girls who were less segregated in their views as some thought proper. One of my first Sundays I had an incident with the Mayor who was a thorough segregationist. It took me some years to make a friend of him, but eventually he was in a room near my Dad's at the Clinic Convalescent Center and welcomed our dog Magic, who I often brought to visit when I went to see Dad.

Our church was an imposing two story brick building on the corner of Main and Broadway, just two blocks from the courthouse. It included an impressive sanctuary with a good pipe organ. There were two overflow rooms off the sanctuary and behind it one or more classrooms. Underneath were the church office, a church school office and several classrooms. Across the street was a fairly new educational building with a large assembly room and stage and some eight or ten classrooms. There was no parking area except on the street, but soon after I arrived the church succeeded in buying an adjacent corner lot which was soon converted for parking. Adjacent to the sanctuary on Broadway was a most attractive office building which had been erected by a law firm only a short time before Judge James Gordon moved his office out of town. The church had considered buying it for its excellent office space and a few places for parking. But they thought the asking price was too high. It seemed to me to be ideal, so I suggested that they offer the owner a more reasonable price. To their amazement he accepted, so only a few months after we arrived in Madisonville that building became an excellent addition to our facilities. It contained an entry office for the secretary, two offices for ministers, a large open room which we used as an attractive parlor, and a small kitchen. The parlor was a real attraction and it was soon decorated beautifully. Upstairs were three large rooms, one equipped for a library. Soon after I arrived Billy Williams, the West Area Minister, came to see me about the possibility of moving the West Area office to Madisonville and wondering if we would rent them rooms in our new office building. The church was quite agreeable, so soon Billy moved to two of the upstairs rooms, which marked the beginning of a long fine relationship both with Billy and the West Area. He soon became one of my strongest supporters and at his suggestion some years later we both started work together on our doctorates at the Vanderbilt University Divinity School.

As soon as we moved into the beautiful new Office Building, we began to settle into a busy routine. Doris Boles was my first secretary and soon I was able to dictate letters and get the church's program active. The church was well organized with working committees for every area of church life. I spent my mornings in the office working on my sermon and correspondence. Charles Blakemore had done a great deal of counseling, and so I soon had many calling at the office for guidance and advice. Most afternoons were devoted to calling on the membership and prospective members. I soon found myself very much involved in hospital and nursing home calling. The hospital at the time we went to Madisonville was fairly large, some four floors. And we had three or more nursing homes—Clinic

Convalescent Center, Kentucky Rest Haven and Senior Citizens. I devoted a great deal of time to these calls and soon became known for the hours I spent at the hospital. Early in my days in Madisonville the church started monthly communion for shut-ins. Both in homes and the hospital many people would be invited to join in communion provided by the elders. Once we had taken communion to any one I would include them on my calling lists. And soon this became a sizable group on which I called regularly. The time came when some members said I roamed the halls of the hospital.

Doris and Jack Boles became long-time friends. Their daughter Martha was close to the same age as Connie and when they grew up, they became very active not only in the youth program of the church but in attendance at regional and national conventions. Husky-voiced Jack played the clarinet in the Community Band directed by Dean Dowdy, the long-time director of the high school band. Jack persisted in getting me to join the band, which I finally did and had several good years playing the drums. Thirty years after playing in the Vanderbilt band, it took me a month before I could follow the music, another month before I could begin to use my sticks, but after three months I began to play acceptably enough that Dean Dowdy never threw his music at me as he had been known to do for his students. We gave regular concerts and I thoroughly enjoyed playing in the community band. I even organized a small band at the church around several members who were also in the band or budding musicians. We played for family night dinners and special occasions, not too well but with lots of enthusiasm.

Doris resigned after a few months as secretary. She was succeeded by Cathy Matheny and after a few months by Ginny Williams. Soon Mary Simms came and told me she would like to be my secretary. This was the beginning of a long relationship with Mary and her husband Kinchloe Simms. At Christmas one year the Simms took the lead in arranging a special gift to us of a full set of the Lenox Christmas china pattern. They had a daughter Diane, who grew up while we were there and eventually married Paul McDougal, who was from Russellville and then ran the bookstore at Western Kentucky University. Many years later when I was doing the interim ministry at the First Christian Church in Bowling Green I called on Diane and her family. During that time Diane died and I was able to baptize her son Matthew. Mary always insisted that I had influenced him to go into the ministry, which he did, for which I was proud. Kinchloe died after a long illness while we were there. Later Mary married Fulton Rucker, whose wife had died of a long illness about the same time as Kinchloe. I was privileged to marry them and saw this develop into a very fine relationship between two people who had both been leaders in their churches. Fulton soon resigned from the Presbyterian Church in order to join Mary in ours.

One of the first couples we got to know were David and Mary Lou Sharp. David was a mail carrier who had grown up in Nebo. He and his parents had been in the Nebo church when Dad had been their pastor, and they moved their membership to Madisonville not long before we came there. They had two daughters, Becky and Anita, who were the age of our girls and became their close friends. They graduated from High School and Anita entered the Community College while I was teaching there, one of the best students I ever had. David was a shade tree mechanic who was a great help to me in keeping our old Vauxhall running until we could buy a better second car. Mary Lou eventually joined the staff of the new Community College and when Carol Lee came home after graduating from the University of Missouri, gave her a job as her assistant in the learning laboratory. This gave Bo the opportunity to work on her master's degree at Western Kentucky University, which she completed in two years.

Thurmon (Jimmy) and Lois Clark befriended us early and gave us much help through all the years. Their daughter Carol was a little older than our girls. Their son Dallas helped his father in the very successful machine equipment service business and later took it over. When we arrived in Madisonville they saw that I needed a good typewriter for my office, so they gave the church a new 400 Royal typewriter. I used it constantly for the twenty years I was in Madisonville. We have continued to have a close relationship with them. Lois is now at the Paragon retirement home in Madisonville; Thurmon died from Alzheimer's at a center near Carol's home in Alabama.

There were several lay ministers in the church when we arrived in Madisonville and we naturally became good friends of all of them. Two were brothers--Roelan and Harold Ledbetter. They both participated regularly in all West Area activities while serving nearby churches through the years. Roelan and Imogene Ledbetter became especially close friends and they continued to see us regularly until Imogene recently passed away. They have two sons. A third lay minister was Roy Schmetzer. He and Betty had four girls, all somewhat near the ages of ours. A fourth was Robert Wilson and later Bill Adcock. After a few years I taught a class for these lay ministers and others in the church who were interested. We gave college credit through Culver-Stockton College. This was a very worthwhile relationship.

One of those who participated in the class was Bill Morton. He and Alice Whayne were not only strong leaders in the church but often participated in conventions. We took them with us to one memorable International Convention which Bill never forgot. They often had us for meals in their home and she was especially nice to the girls, planning interesting things for them to do when we came to visit.

Dayton and Eleanor Stinnett took a strong interest in us. Dayton was a retired electrician and Eleanor was a fine English teacher who had the girls in her classes. They loved to eat out and often invited us to go with them to Charley's restaurant which was near Fort Campbell. Nothing was too good for them and they encouraged us to eat the finest steaks and other delectables. They developed a special interest in Carol Lee and Connie, who was not averse to ordering anything on the menu. One day Dayton asked Connie why she hadn't ordered the specialty, Charley's Treat. Connie said it was because her sister had poked her under the table and told her not to order anything that expensive. Not long after Dayton died, Eleanor went with us on one of our overseas tours.

As noted earlier, we had acquired our little Chihuahua, Snoopy, just before leaving Kirksville. He often slept with Carol and me under the covers at our feet. He was a fine traveler and went with us to many camps in the Lake of the Ozarks. Clyde and Lorena Ruby lived next door to us with two very large dogs. Snoopy loved to play with them and could find a hole in the fence to go next door. One day the Ruby's called to tell us that Snoopy had been badly hurt and was at their front door. They thought the dogs had killed him, but I always thought he had gotten caught in a fence and the dogs had brought him up to the Ruby's house. I got him cleaned up and was looking for a wooden box in which to bury him when Fred Strother at he funeral home offered us a baby casket which had been damaged. So we were able to take Snoopy to be buried in a beautiful casket in what would become the pet cemetery in Russellville. It now includes the graves of seven of our family dogs and four cats which Mother and Dad had given a home.

Soon we had another little dog Muffin, that friends gave us, but after a few days she was killed by a car. But we would soon acquire another greatly loved dog, Magic. Cathie had had Magic while she was in school at Murray. Cathie left her with a friend the next summer who let her out and she roamed the streets of Murray, getting pregnant before Cathie could retrieve her. She brought her to us so we soon had seven beautiful puppies. We were able to find friends to adopt them, but Magic lived with us for sixteen years. She loved to travel and went with us camping and visiting our family all over the country. When she saw us packing she would lie at the rear wheels of the car so that we could not leave without her. We took her with us to Canada and to Mexico. She moved with us to Russellville when we retired and enjoyed our yard. One morning we found her in the doorway to the dining room where she obviously had tried to get to us before she died.

During our first year in our new church we developed a number of activities that would continue through the years. We started a very exciting School of World Outreach each spring, using different countries each year. And we originated Youth Outreach Tours, taking a bus load of young people on a week long visit of our church's outreach institutions. The first one went to Indianapolis. We started a Christmas Eve communion service our first year. We inherited a beautiful Last Supper Portrayal, which was directed for years by Imogene Ledbetter. It was a live depiction of daVinci's Last Supper. Jesus and the twelve disciples had speaking parts. Each year the sanctuary was filled for this beautiful communion service.

Sermon preparation used much of my time each week. I used the lectionary which each week recommended Old and New Testament and Psalm scriptures from which to choose sermon texts. I would announce my topic in the newsletter and spend several days thinking through the ideas for my sermon. By Saturday I would type out the sermon, often late that night. I never went into the pulpit without having my sermon written out. I have a long shelf of sermons at home as the result of this practice. Counseling occupied much of my time each week. Weddings, especially church ones, and funerals were an important part of my days. I gave much individual attention to every funeral and soon became known for my handling of the services.

Of course, church membership was very important, so we conducted many visitation campaigns and each year I had membership classes for children and adults, usually leading up to Easter. Dr. Charles Fisher was our family physician. He and I were born on the same day and year, so we often celebrated our birthdays together. He had not responded to our efforts to get him into our church membership along with his wife Iris. The Fishers had adopted two boys, and the younger one, Chuck, came forward at the invitation one Sunday. To my surprise Dr. Fisher came with him, and I was privileged to baptize father and son. Chuck was handicapped but did remarkable things with his hands, modeling figures. We have one of the beautiful dolls he gave us. And he made a complete set of Nativity figures which we used on the communion table every Christmas. Dr. Fisher years later gave the money for a spire to complete our new building in my honor several years after I retired.

We badly needed someone to work with our religious education program. Soon we called Mildred Slack who had just graduated from Lexington Theological Seminary. Millie brought much new life to our church school and youth program. She played a guitar and soon had organized a group of folksingers which developed the long tradition of the West Wind that sang regularly in church services and for many outside groups. This included several young people playing their guitars along with songs of the protest period, which caused some concern by a few church members. But they soon won strong approval. Millie was also responsible for the Coffee House we started on Friday nights on the stage of the Educational Building.

During this time I preached for another revival at Dad's church, Dogwood near Hopkinsville. I directed a CYF Conference at Kum-ba-ya in which Carol also taught. And I started another tradition by serving as the chaplain at the Hillman Ferry Campground in the Land Between the Lakes. We spent a week each summer, enjoying a trailer provided for us while we visited campers and conducted a church service on Sunday morning. This continued throughout our years at Madisonville, at the various camps.

During the first year we were in Madisonville there was a city-wide revival led by Ford Philpott. I was very much involved and got to know him quite well. He was promoting a trip to the Holy Land the next year and some of our members decided that we should go. They made up the expenses of the trip and sent us for what would prove to be our first overseas adventure. It was a good experience. We spent two weeks in Jerusalem while Philpott led a revival with services each night. It came at a time when there was much violence, so Jerusalem was well guarded. We knew that there were guards walking on the roof of our hotel at night. But we had no incidents. Carol and I saw all the sights of the Holy City and parts of Israel. We saw the tomb of David, the site of the Upper Room, walked the Via Dolorosa, the site of the crucifixion, and the garden tomb of Jesus. Lois Clark was with us on the tour and one day she accompanied us when we rented a cab driver to take us on a trip south from Jerusalem to the end of Israel at Beersheba. He drove us past Hebron, which was so dangerous that he would not go in, just pointed it out to us, and then all the way south. It had been said that Israel extended from Dan in the north to Beersheba at the southern tip of Palestine and I wanted to see as much of it as possible. From Beersheba we went back around the Gaza strip to the Mediterranean coast where we had lunch and then up through the orange country along the coast back up to Jerusalem.

One day our group was taken to Caesarea northwest of Jerusalem. While there on the ocean we were watching the waves come in and one came so close that Miss Kate Todd, who was from Madisonville, jumped back and fell, breaking her hip. There we were some forty or more miles from Jerusalem so they put Miss Kate on the back seat of the bus to get her back to the city. I was not in charge of the tour group, but since she was from my home town they asked me to take care of her. Since it was a Friday the Jewish hospitals were closed and we had to take her to a French hospital in Jerusalem. I went to see her regularly and contacted her sons back in the states. The doctors said it would be better for us to get her home rather than convalescing in Jerusalem for several weeks. They said they would arrange for her to be transported in a cast. Her son had made arrangements for her to be flown home, leaving the same day we were to leave with our group. I went with her in an ambulance to the plane in Tel Aviv. I had been involved in the plan to fly her to New York where her son would meet her. When we got to the airport, they said she couldn't fly without having made arrangements for two seats. I spent some time arguing with them, but finally got them to agree to let her fly. I went with her to her plane and up on a lift to get her in the upper nose of the plane. But by that time the pilot was about to take off and I just barely got back on the ground. All that time I had the tickets for our group flying to Athens. I just barely got back to the terminal in time for us all to take off.

The next year the Philpott group asked me to recruit passengers for a trip to the Holy Land again. This meant that Carol and I would be able to fly without cost. When we succeeded, we took our first Tour Group to Europe, something that Carol and I sponsored many times in the years to come.

When we left Kirksville I had almost completed work on a Master's degree, majoring in guidance in the College of Education at Northeast Missouri. I only lacked four hours of required work. So in our first summer at Madisonville I enrolled at the University of Evansville, taking two courses that I needed. These were soon transferred back to Northeast and at the next commencement I received my Master's degree.

One of the first events after we had settled in at Madisonville was the regional assembly of the Christian Church in Kentucky at Owensboro. In a business session I made a plea for more support of the churches in West Kentucky. Obviously it caught some attention, for soon I was elected to the state board. This was the beginning of many years in various positions on the CCK Board, eventually leading to a two year term as President of the Christian Church in Kentucky. That involved dozens of trips to Lexington through those years in Madisonville.

Farris Clifton was the head of the Christian Church Homes of Kentucky. He came to visit me often and eventually asked me to serve on the Board of the Homes. We were just starting the campus of the Hopkinsville home, and I was involved in its work when we erected the first building of the campus. After it was well established, I kept insisting that we needed a chaplain. After I had pestered them enough they finally called a part-time chaplain, which was the beginning of a long line of chaplains in our homes. I continued to serve on the national Board for sixteen years, spending some of that time in the promotional work. This meant many trips to Louisville for Board meetings as well as on the developing campuses. Some years later, due to the work of Russellville Mayor Wallace Herndon, a fund was raised to provide for a Chapel in the Hopkinsville home in honor of my father, the Edward Coffman Memorial Chapel.

One of the most original things I did in Madisonville was starting the Pastor's Stay-to-Church Club. Boys and girls were invited to enroll in a program of Church School and church attendance during a twelve week period. Each one received a booklet in which to record their attendance and keep a record of each worship service. Two elders were to confirm their attendance. Those satisfactorily completing the program were given a special trip. The first year it was to Mammoth Cave, but soon it became a day at Opryland in Nashville. This was looked forward to annually and was always a great adventure. We took them on the church van and enjoyed the trip. Opryland was in its heyday, with wonderful rides and outstanding musical shows throughout the day. Carol and I especially enjoyed the shows while the kids kept the rides busy. This was something which I repeated at some of my interim ministries with great success.

Not long after we got started in Madisonville several parents in the church asked Carol to start a pre-school program. They knew of her having worked with one in Kirksville and her college training in this field. In the fall of 1967 Carol started the First Christian Church Nursery School with six three-and four-year old boys and girls. This was the beginning of twenty great years. Very soon many more children in the church were involved in the Nursery School and then many from other churches asked to be included. Carol was a wonderful story-teller, taught great songs and games, used many techniques to help her children learn the alphabet, the rudiments of writing and reading, and love of good books. Each year at Christmas and the end of school she had great programs to which she invited the families of her students to display their accomplishments with songs and skits. By the time she retired she had over a hundred children each year in her Nursery School, with several helpers. She enjoyed seeing many of her first children grow up to graduate from high school. The dental therapist, Hannah Dugger, who cleaned her teeth in recent years was one of her four-year old Nursery School students.

One day Carol took Connie with her shopping. Connie was wearing what we often called her "uniform," blue jeans, boots and a sweat shirt. Carol asked Connie why she didn't like to wear frilly skirts like most girls did when they went to town. Connie said, "Well, Mom, it's like this. I may see some boys, or I may need to run fast, or I may want to throw a ball, so I have to be prepared."

During our days in Columbia I had been quite active in Scouting. All through my ministry I supported the Boy Scout movement by being involved in the units that our church sponsored, involved with the Cub Scout program, and making a special emphasis on Scout Sundays. During part of this time I served as Cubmaster for the Pack which the Madisonville church sponsored. This required regular meeting times and promotion of Council projects. But I was also involved in the district Councils. This eventually led to week long training programs at the Philmont Scout Ranch in New Mexico while we were in Madisonville. At the first one I was sent for training in administration. This was a fine experience for our whole family. We lived in a tent with a floor, and had our meals in the dining room at the Center. There was an excellent program of activities for all the members of the family. While I was in training sessions each day, Carol and the girls all had many craft programs and expeditions to explore. The next year I was in a workshop for training with the God and Country program. That time we enjoyed buffalo-burgers, a regular treat from the herd of buffalo on the Scout Ranch. A week at Philmont was always one that we treasured.

In the spring of 1968 I received an invitation to participate in a fine program at the Ecumenical Continuing Education Center for a ten day conference in Michigan. Custice Fletcher of the Episcopal Church had nominated me and we went together to the conference for a great experience. Interestingly enough, the invitation had come from Parker Rossman of the Center at Yale. Parker would continue to be a close friend through the years.

Cathie found her last years in high school at Madisonville-North Hopkins some different from Kirksville. She was not so well known and had to make new friends. Among those were Sandy Pasco, Fonda Austen, Denise Edwards and Mary Johnson She found a boy friend Mike Crick of Earlington, who played in a band on weekends. Cathie spent much time listening to his music. And her friendship with Mike followed her into college at Murray. Cathie kept up her friendship with Sandy and Fonda. Years later when Carol had been so ill, they came to visit us in Russellville. Cathie was an excellent musician. She played the piano and was quite well accepted in Dean Dowdy's high school band. He used her not only on the clarinet but at times on the bass clarinet. She sang in Ruth Williams' Glee Club.

Her senior year in high school Cathie, like her parents, went to the United Nations Seminar in New York and Washington. We took her with us to New York but left her at the hotel the day we left for an overseas trip. She went to see "Fiddler On he Roof" and met Ann Ray Martin who got her to her hotel. At eighteen, she was left on her own overnight in the city before joining the Seminar.

Cathie was so much involved in music that when it came time to select the college she would attend, she was interested in visiting only one school. She said she wanted to major in music and Murray was by far the best school for that purpose. So she started as a freshman at Murray State University. Strangely enough, she never took a music course at Murray but became very much interested in psychology. So by the time she graduated from Murray she had majored in social work. Cathie was Vice-president of the Panhellenic Council, President of the Social

Work Club, and initiated into Alpha Chi, the top honor society for scholarship at Murray. She was included in Who's Who Among American Universities and Colleges. Her junior year she was accepted as a Social Work Intern, and worked with Mary Morse in the Hopkinsville Public Assistance Office. She was able to repeat this the next year and had the same job in the Madisonville office. Looking toward a Master's degree, she found that Florida State University had the best opportunity, so she applied at FSU and was offered a good scholarship. But while at Murray Cathie had become quite interested in Mitchell McCandless. She and Butch were married the day after she graduated from Murray and moved to Tallahassee for Cathie to work on her Master's. This started a new direction in their lives. Butch had lived on Kentucky Lake with his parents and was an outstanding swimmer. He used that ability in connection with his work as a millwright and underwater diver to secure quite remunerative jobs. Together they lived comfortably while Cathie finished her degree. Then she started working with Hillsborough Community Mental Health Center in Tampa and later with the Northside Mental Health Center and the VA Hospital in Tampa. They stayed in Temple Terrace, during this time. But after a time Butch and Cathie got a divorce. And in the process Cathie bought a condo in Lake Forrest. Subsequently she had discovered an opportunity to work for the U. S. Department of the Army in Germany. When she was accepted she moved to Wurtzburg where she lived for nearly three years while she conducted drug counseling clinics for the Army. She bought a car and traveled over much of Europe while there. Carol and I spent a week with her when she took us over much of southern Germany Cathie began to do a great deal of running and ran in the French Marathon in Paris. She also became a skiing addict and spent much time on the slopes of Garmish and in Italy and Switzerland. The last year in Germany she was moved to Wildflecken very near the German border.

 After returning from Germany Cathie worked at the VA Hospital in Tampa and then went into private practice, and lived in her condo with Carol Lee. It was at this time that she met Dr. Peter Paluch, who was teaching at the University of South Florida. After they were married Peter accepted a position with Hartwick College in Oneonta, New York. So they left sunny Florida to begin a new life in upstate New York where their two children, Stefanie Carol and Peter Jacob were born. Soon after the move Cathie established a private practice in psychiatric social work with an office downtown in Oneonta.

 Carol Lee entered the seventh grade at the Junior High School on Seminary. She soon became very active in many ways and acquired many good friends: Becky Sharp, Becky Clements, Jamie Hargrove, and Georgia Terry. We still laugh over the time when Bo invited Becky Clements to spend the night with her. Becky's mother wasn't sure since she didn't know Carol Lee's parents. When she learned that her father was a minister, she decided that it was all right. Becky became not only one of her best friends through the years, but Carol Lee worked at Clements Jewelry through her high school years and later. She also worked at the Main Street pizza house, the VFW concession stand, and the gift shop at the hospital The next year at Madisonville-North Hopkins Carol Lee joined Dean Dowdy's band, playing the flute, and Ruth Williams' Glee Club. She was always afraid when she was in the marching band that she would turn right when the band was turning left. When Cathie graduated, Bo told her that she was going to drop out of the band. I told her that if she did, she must tell Dean Dowdy. It took her a year to get up the nerve to do so. Bo was in Rainbow Girls and active in CYF.

Carol Lee was a good student, but she was a little hesitant about the SAT and other tests important for college acceptance. In fact, her advisor, Mrs. Summers, once told her that she was not a good candidate for college work. This was a strange judgment on a young woman who would eventually graduate from Columbia College, the University of Missouri and receive a Master's degree from Western Kentucky University.

After graduating from Madisonville-North Hopkins Carol Lee went to Columbia for two years, working toward the Associate of Arts at Columbia College, the successor to Christian College where her mother had graduated. She had an excellent experience there, living in the Hughes Hall dormitory, serving one year as president. She worked as the receptionist at the dorm. Her friends included Diana Williams Turner and Cindy Schwartzerfeger Abduson.

When she graduated from Columbia College Carol Lee entered the University of Missouri for her next two years. She majored in elementary education. She did her practice teaching at Field Elementary and Rock Bridge Elementary schools. This was a good time for her, living near her grandparents. Frank and Lenora took good care of her, feeding her often and helping get her to school on occasion. She worked hard on a very low budget. She worked in the University library and she often worked till midnight at Pagliai's Pizza. It was a great occasion when Mother and Dad joined us in celebrating her graduation from MU.

After graduating Carol Lee returned home and soon found a job working in the Learning Lab at Madisonville Community College with Mary Lou Sharp. This was helping students who were deficient in certain needed areas. While there she worked on a Master's degree at Western Kentucky University, taking weekend courses, and received her degree in Educational Counseling. When Carol and I were visiting Cathie in Tampa we noticed an ad for a position with a college in Florida. We suggested it to Carol Lee and she followed it up, joining the faculty of Pasco Hernando Community College in Newport Richey, Florida. It was close to Tampa so she lived with Cathie and drove to her school.

This led to her next position as Director of Financial Aid at Erwin Vo-Tec, part of the Hillsborough County School System. From there she went to Florida Federal Savings and Loan as Vice-President of Marketing, then to Wachovia Bank. This move took her to San Francisco, where she eventually became President and CEO of Chela Financial Resources, a student loan originator and secondary market. Carol Lee grew this company from three employees and $300 million in total assets to over 180 employees and $2.8 billion in total assets. In 1994 Carol Lee decided to move from San Francisco to the warmer climate of Mill Valley where she bought her home at 261 Perry Street. Everyone came to help her celebrate her move into the house and her fortieth birthday.

Leaving a good school and a neighborhood with many friends, Connie Sue needed a little time to get adjusted to a new school and living with no children in the neighborhood Thanks to Sissy Finley, her second grade teacher at Hall Street Elementary School, she soon was much involved in her new life in Madisonville. She had excellent teachers, Dot Bacon in the third grade, then Mrs. Poole in the fourth, and Mrs. Pruitt in the fifth. She was a Brownie Scout, selling Girl Scout cookies. Artie Mae Strother amazed her when she bought one of every variety of cookies. Connie was a Girl Scout and received the God and Community badge. She served on the school patrol and was in the extended program in the fourth and fifth grades. She helped build a village of matchbooks.

Moving to the sixth grade at Seminary Street School, Connie was on the student council and announced the morning devotions one week on the PA system. She was in the glee club and played her cello in the school orchestra. We had bought the cello for her from Harold Epperson's music store in Kirksville. She played it on through High School. Middle School was great for Connie, but she hit her stride at Madisonville-North Hopkins. She was an excellent student and got involved in every activity possible. She was in Tri-Hi-Y, the glee club, the orchestra, Beta Club, on the annual staff. She ran track until she hurt her knee and had to have two surgeries. That knee would plague her for years. And of course she played soft ball whenever possible. Connie was the manager/statistician for the basketball team three years and manager/statistician of the baseball team. When she graduated with top honors, she soon won an excellent scholarship at the University of Southern California in Los Angeles. We never knew why she decided on USC but thought it had something to do with the opportunity to see Rose Bowl games because of its excellent football teams. And she did—twice. In her third year at USC she was accepted for the "Sacramento Semester" by the School of Public Administration and was looking forward to the Rose Bowl game between USC and Michigan. Connie had a good experience in college and met her future husband. She was engaged to Bill Burke, who had been a student at Southern Cal.

When Connie received her B.S. degree in public administration at USC she left immediately for three weeks in Germany with Cathie and spent time touring Europe, returning home to prepare for her wedding. Connie and Bill Burke married in our new sanctuary in Madisonville with all the Burke clan and her sisters involved. Connie's grandfather, Pyke Coffman, and her Uncle Henry Campbell conducted the ceremony. After a honeymoon in Hawaii they moved to Chico, in northern California, helping Bill's sister run Honey Run Farm. They came to attend the World's Fair in Knoxville with us and Carol Lee. Connie got a job with a company in Chico and soon acquired two dogs, Trojan and Kegger. Things had been going well until she was being abused and one time almost killed by Bill. Connie left home immediately with her dogs, never to return alone. She continued to work in Chico while she got her divorce. She worked for a time, living in a primitive farm home and then in a house in an almond grove. But with the encouragement of her company she finally decided to return to school and moved to Nashville to work on an MBA in the Owen School of Management at Vanderbilt University. She bought a home where she could keep Trojan and Kegger while in school.

When Connie finished her MBA in 1987 she went to work for Oscar Mayer in Madison, Wisconsin. She lived on a farm with her dogs and had an unusual experience in learning to gut hogs as part of her work. After a year she moved to the Louis Rich plant in Modesto, California, where she was human resources manager. She applied for a position with Bridgestone Tires and soon moved to McMinnville, Tennessee where the new plant would be. Carol and I went to McMinnville to scout out possibilities for a new home which she soon bought on Chambers Street, moving with Trojan and Kegger. It was there as human resources manager that she met Ed Hitchcock, an electrical engineer.

Carol was very much involved in the life of the community. She always kept in touch with Madisonville-North Hopkins High School while the girls were there and was soon elected President of the PTA, able to give support in many ways. The year that Carol Lee was a senior there was an incident in which Carol was very much involved. Just before the Prom there had been a racial fight among several students, which prompted the school to cancel the Prom. This disturbed the students, especially the black kids who were in the center during this time of racial unrest. Carol went to see the principal, Floyd Brown, to try to get the Prom reinstated. She didn't succeed, but she was able to work out a plan by which the Prom could be held at the Armory, off school property. With the help of several parents Carol arranged for it all and announced an Open House to be held at our home on Park Avenue before the Prom. All went well and that night we had dozens of students, black and white, streaming into our house before the Prom. Carol had lovely refreshments and we had a great evening thanks to her work

Billy Williams and I had become good friends from the time we went to Madisonville. He was the West Area Minister, just establishing this excellent program for our churches. As noted, after we acquired the new office building he asked if the West Area could use two of our upstairs rooms for their offices. This was the beginning of several very satisfying years when we worked together. Bill and I shared many trips through those years when we both went to Board meetings and other activities of the Christian Church in Kentucky. One day Bill asked me if I would be interested in joining him in working on a doctorate at Vanderbilt. I readily agreed and for the year of 1971-72 we shared a bed at the Disciples House while we worked on our degrees. We used half a room with another student. I was usually there the first two or three days of the week and he would be there the last days. We kept a bedroll in case we both had to be there at the same time.

I worked hard that year while I continued my pastoral duties at the church. I felt I had to finish my degree in a year because Cathie and Carol Lee would both be in college the next fall and we couldn't afford for all of us to be in school at the same time. The Dean of the Divinity School wasn't sure I could do it in one school year. But I already had some credits built up before I started and took the maximum hours I could each semester. It was a close call, but I was able to complete my dissertation in time to have it published before commencement. Dr. Herman Norton was my major professor and he supervised my work in addition to teaching several of my courses. I had one course with Dr. Eugene deSelle in which a young man by the name of Al Gore was quite vocal. Al's parents were Vanderbilt graduates and strong supporters of the Divinity School. Years later Al would serve eight years as Vice-President of the United State with President Bill Clinton and would be very narrowly defeated for President even when winning the majority vote in the nation, and George W. Bush became President. It was a great day when my family and friends came to help me celebrate graduation from the Vanderbilt Divinity School with a Doctor of Ministry degree. At the same time Carol Lee was graduating from High School, so we had our pictures made together in our caps and gowns.

Carol and I were involved for three years in the Southern Academy of Teaching at Craig Springs, West Virginia that gave us outstanding experience in sensitivity training. Billy and Shirley Williams were also involved in this summer weeklong experience. Carol and I both gained a great deal from it, but she more than I, for which I was thankful.

Even more important was our Emmaus experience. Jim Ashmore insisted that I come with him to a weekend Walk to Emmaus that was sponsored by the Methodist Church in Nashville. Emmaus was an intensive time of training for growth in churchmanship through lectures, devotional experiences and life rededication. It was a very moving time for me, as it was also for Carol when she made the Walk two weeks later. We got many of our church members involved, and Carol and I worked numerous times on Emmaus Walk teams. Before we retired something like eighty of our members had made Emmaus Walks, and many more of them continue to be active in this fine program. It left a big impact on our congregation. Several years ago the name was changed to the Big Banquet, but the idea is essentially the same. Later Carol and I helped to start the Emmaus program in Bowling Green and when we were doing the interim ministry in Bowling Green we both served on teams for the Emmaus Walks.

In July of 1975, lightning struck our sanctuary on Main and Broadway, burning it to the ground. We were at the Land Between the Lakes where I was serving as chaplain for a week. When they called us late on Saturday night to tell us the church was burning, they suggested that we stay till I could have the Sunday morning worship at the campground. As soon as it was over we rushed home to find water still being poured on the remnants of the sanctuary. The church was having a worship service in the social hall of the Educational Building when we arrived. Connie, having watched the church burn the night before, soon was helping to retrieve what was left in the basement of the old sanctuary. This was the beginning of a long period of four years until we could decide where and how to rebuild.

Carol began to make a name for herself with her annual Lenten Luncheons. She worked on them for a long time before Lent, deciding on a theme and working up supportive decorations. At the luncheon she would give a beautiful devotion as she set the theme for the observance of Lent. This was looked forward to with great interest each year.

1979 was a difficult year for us. Mother died at our home as a result of a heart attack in March. We had had a delightful time the night before, recalling many good days in the past. We took her home to Russellville for the service at the church which she had served so many years. In the spring Lenora had eye surgery with difficulty recovering. Dad fell at home and broke his hip, spending some time convalescing at the Christian Heath Center in Hopkinsville. Then in November Frank died suddenly of a heart attack. This meant our family group was much smaller at Christmas. But Cathie came home from Tampa where she was working at the VA Hospital and teaching courses in assertiveness training. Carol Lee was living with her while she finished her first semester as Guidance Counselor at Pasco-Hernandez Community College in Port Richey, Florida.

By 1980 we had finally completed construction of our new church on College Avenue at North Main Street after almost five years deciding on the new location, making plans and raising the money. It was a beautiful building with entrances at ground level. The dedication service was a great day with warm response from the entire community.

The building of the new church had been accomplished with relatively little difficulty, but there were two or three people who created problems. The architect had designed the sanctuary with rounded pews and elevated pulpit and lectern so that everyone could see well. A unique feature was the use of the communion table in the center of the rows so that we "gathered round" it when we observed the Lord's Supper. Two or three members tried to change this plan, wanting to put the table across the front. I insisted that we follow the architect's plan, but in the process created some enmity which was never forgotten. This resentment continued for some time until I learned that they were trying to have me leave. It came to a head at a Board meeting in 1981 when three women stood up to ask for my resignation. The only reason they gave was that seven years is ordinarily as long as most ministers stay in a church and I had been there fourteen years, so it was time for me to go. What they planned had become known so there was a tremendous group at the Board meeting. Over a hundred came so that the meeting had to be held in the sanctuary. I simply sat there and listened as many people came to my defense. Dr. Keith Bachman was one of my strongest supporters. A woman told me that she had never spoken in public before but she just had to stand up and support me. No action was taken that night and the next day Billy Williams took me to lunch to tell me that after what had happened I could stay there the rest of my life if I wished to do so. Actually I stayed for six more years before I made the decision on my own to retire.

The next year was very important for Carol and me as we made our Emmaus Walks, the "shortcut in Christianity." It had a great influence on the life of our congregation. Carol Lee, Connie and Bill joined us for a week at the World's Fair in Knoxville, Tennessee. And then Carol and I finally got to visit Cathie in Wurzburg, spending two weeks in Germany, France and Austria. Carol Lee joined us for a few days before we returned home with stops in Paris and London. During this time Carol and I worked a good deal on the Russellville home. With Dad in the Clinic Convalescent Center in Madisonville, we let the Art Guild use the Coffman home for their meetings and exhibits. They helped us do some much needed improvements.

Grandmother Alexander had not been well so Carol brought her home to Madisonville. Bo and Connie were home for Easter and Lenora talked with Cathie in Germany before she quietly slipped away. After the funeral in Columbia we spent some time closing her home and ending the Alexander period of our lives.

We continued improving the home in Russellville where the Art Guild held an Open House during the Tobacco Festival, with many of Mother's paintings on display. Connie and Bo came home from California for Christmas in time to greet Cathie returning home after three and a half years in Germany.

On June 5th, 1984 Carol and I celebrated our thirty-fifth wedding anniversary. Then in August we led a tour group to Europe for the 350th celebration of the Passion Play in Oberammergau. Connie joined us as we went from Amsterdam, Brussels and Cologne before a trip down the Rhine to Frankfurt, through the Black Forest to Lucerne, Zurich and Lichtenstein. That fall the church celebrated the fortieth anniversary of my ordination to the Christian ministry. The girls all came to share in this very meaningful event. We acquired another dog when my cousin, Evelyn Long Riley, sent her little schnauzer Mary Poppins to live with us. She and Magic became great friends.

1985 was a year of transition. Cathie established her own mental health counseling service, with an office in Dunedin, Florida; Carol Lee became a financial aid representative for a bank in St. Petersburg.; and Connie moved to Nashville to work on an MBA degree in the Owen School of Management at Vanderbilt University. Jo Wagner joined our church staff as secretary along with Mary Simms. Carol and I attended the General Assembly of the Christian Church in Des Moines, Iowa.

When Connie moved to Nashville she bought a home at 5300 Elkins Ave, where she lived comfortably with her dogs Trojan and Kegger. This was helped by Mother's will for $10,000 to the three girls and some to Beth Campbell. Connie used her portion for the down payment on her home as had Cathie when she bought her condo in Lutz and Carol Lee doing the same in Tampa.

In 1986 Carol Lee made a major change in her life when she moved to San Francisco managing the Student Loan office for Wachovia Bank, CHELA. Cathie's private practice was growing and Connie was well on the way to her MBA at Vanderbilt. We had Open House at the parsonage for a farewell Christmas celebration. Dad was able to come for our last Christmas in Madisonville from the Clinic Convalescent Center.

It was not easy to leave Madisonville after twenty wonderful years where our girls had gone through school, college and marriages. But the warm outpouring of love that our people showered upon us helped us to leave with great appreciation for all that had happened in those years. We had lots of help in moving to Russellville where we had already spent several months in remodeling the Coffman home for our new life there.

First Christian Church, Madisonville, Kentucky

Parsonage in Madisonville

Easter in Madisonville

Carol and Ed Enjoy a Moment

25th Wedding Anniversary

25th Wedding Anniversary with our Parents

Celebrating 40 Years in the Ministry

Travels in Egypt

In the Vanderbilt
Homecoming Band

7

The Interim Years

Before we had hardly moved to Russellville we had to leave immediately for a tour group to Europe. We had thirty-eight people going with us to Ireland, Wales, Scotland and England., ending with two days in London. Then Carol and I attended the General Assembly of the Christian Church in Louisville. And soon I was doing supply preaching in nearby churches.

Before we retired in Madisonville we had been making plans to return to my home in Russellville. We contracted with Mr. Chapman to make some changes in the house and add a carport. We asked him if we could add seventeen more feet to the rear of the house which was already like a freight train, with five rooms having been built on behind the original two story brick front. He asked why we wanted to build more on that big old house We told him that that big old house had only one bathroom and one closet. We needed more. So we added a laundry room, closets, a bathroom with tub and shower, and a small side porch. In the process we had to do considerable remodeling in the front of the house. Our request for a carport turned into a large building with outside room for two cars and much needed storage space.

Carol dearly loved her Kentucky home and she made it her own. In the living room we used the two cherry tables that had been a part of my grandmother's dining room table and two of the three armoires which were in the house. One we used for a bookcase and the other for a closet and sound system. Also my grandfather's large desk and my sister's cedar chest which Mother and Dad had had made for her clothes and other treasures when she died. We used several walnut pieces of furniture from the Hill family home, including a chest of drawers, a sugar chest, three end tables and several chairs. Also the big antique family clock which was one of Mother's extensive collection. We bought two matching sofas and a coffee table for the center of he room. Then we brought two large chairs, lamps and pictures from Madisonville. Over the Adam mantle and open fireplace we left the large oil painting of an old castle which my Aunt Lizzie had made. We moved the cast-iron bathtub out of the adjoining bath upstairs to go in our new bath and closet. In the front hall we used our lovely maple secretary with the antique love seat from the Coffman home.

In the dining room we had the mahogany dining table, buffet and china cabinet refinished. David Corbin did a beautiful job on them On the wall with pictures of my ancestors is one of Mother's antique clocks, this an unusual two-faced one. We redid the kitchen with built in cabinets, table-top stove and oven, dishwasher, sink and microwave. We used another of our maple hutches there also. In the family room we used the maple dining set from home and bought a new sofa which folds out to make a bed, something we always use when the family are all here. We also included the restored pie safe which became the home of Carol's growing Christmas village houses. We furnished the two back bedrooms with beds and chests from Grandmother's and family pieces. Upstairs we made a very cozy bedroom with our original maple furniture around the fireplace, with three chests of drawers, maple and antique With our new closet and bath this made a most comfortable home for us for many years until we eventually had to move downstairs because of failing health problems. In the upstairs hall we used a desk we found there, plus chests we had brought with us to outfit a very comfortable office with typewriter and computer, which Carol and the girls had given me on retirement. Later I built a larger computer table with the help of James Gant.

Carol soon had our new home beautifully decorated and began to use seasonal effects. By our first Christmas she had made the Coffman home a real showplace We added many new decorations to those already left by Mother and Dad. The Simpich carolers dominated the living room as they do to this day. And we went to great lengths to secure a ten foot live tree for the front hall. Carol and I were soon active in the First Christian Church, serving as elders.

The girls all came home for Christmas--Cathie with her friend Peter Paluch from Florida, Carol Lee from her work with Wachovia Bank in San Francisco, and Connie from Oscar Mayer in Madison, Wisconsin. We had brought Granddaddy Pyke home from Madisonville but after a few months because of the difficulty of getting help, he moved to the Auburn Nursing Home, ten miles away. He was able to celebrate Christmas with us, but he died two days later at the age of 97. In keeping with family tradition we had visitation at home and went to the church he loved for the memorial service. In accord with his wishes, I spoke for his funeral and Connie sang "The "Holy City."

When we left Madisonville we settled at our family home in Russellville for a life of leisure. But little did we know what lay ahead of us. In the spring of 1988 I was asked to do an interim ministry in Middlesboro, Kentucky. This would be the first of seven very satisfying interims in the next few years. We had an excellent experience in Middlesboro, serving the First Christian Church and living in the parsonage. We were new to Eastern Kentucky so we climbed the mountain trails and explored the hollows of this part of our state. I worked in the community, making many calls and serving on the Board of the Community Assistance office. We made many new friends, among them Hugh and Ave Hite, Homer Hoe (a Phi Kappa Psi fraternity brother) and Larry and Karen Blondell, the musicians who have followed us through the years, singing at Carol's funeral and for other occasions in Russellville. I met Neil Gordon Barry, the four year old grandson of Neil and Tooney Barry when he started coming to church with his parents. I was teaching the Men's Sunday School class and would see him outside my door. I had a funeral for the uncle of Tooney and we went to their home after the service. Neil Gordon came in and took his grandmother's hand, telling her "God is here!" Neil Gordon years later went to Transylvania University where he distinguished himself by supporting a foreign student who was about to be deported. We were sitting quietly at home one night when a tornado hit Middlesboro. It damaged the airport a few blocks from us and much of the downtown area, including some damage to our church. On Sunday morning I preached a sermon on "God Rides the Storm" (Karen Blondell remembered the title). We had a most satisfying time in our first interim ministry, and it was with regret that we returned home at Halloween after nine months.

Cathie and Peter Paluch were married at Thanksgiving, November 26,1988 in Tamps with both families involved in this time of great joy. Carol Lee was maid of honor, Connie sang, and I officiated. They all came home for Christmas—Cathie from her mental health practice and Peter from the University of South Florida, where he was an assistant professor, Carol Lee from the California Higher Education Loan Authority in San Francisco and Connie from the Louis Rich plant in Modesto, California.

1989 was a year of transition for our family. Carol and I started with a Caribbean cruise with her cousin Reda and Dan Whitledge. We very soon moved to Huntsvillle, Alabama for another very satisfying interim ministry at the First Christian Church. The congregation had been divided over the leaving of a much loved pastor under some pressure. We were able to help unite them with much listening and love. Huntsville is an exciting place as the space center, and we had some very interesting experiences, including an evening at the Space Center when the Symphony Orchestra played and they celebrated the twentieth anniversary of the landing on the moon. The three astronauts from that event were there and spoke in person. We made many good friends, among them Chris and Sue Christianson who took us under their wing and remain close to this day. Sue took Carol to antique spots all over Alabama. Just as we were closing our apartment, Huntsville was struck by a devastating tornado which damaged much of the area between our home and the church.

We were all together at the quaint Bavarian style village of Helen, Georgia where we spent a week celebrating our fortieth wedding anniversary. In August Cathie and Peter Paluch moved to upstate New York at Oneonta where Peter accepted a position as a professor at Hartwick College. Cathie established a new practice in mental health counseling while also doing some teaching at the state college. Connie moved from California to Tennessee where she handled human relations for the new Bridgestone Tire plant at Morrison near McMinnville, where she bought a home on Chambers Street and lived with her dogs Trojan and Kegger. Carol Lee was still with CHELA in San Francisco but she survived the disastrous earthquake that damaged much of the city, grateful that her home was not damaged. Carol and I attended the Regional Assembly of the Christian Church in Alabama and the General Assembly in Indianapolis. We spent Thanksgiving with Carol Lee and her dog Benson in San Francisco. But we were all home for Christmas in Russellville.

At all of our interim ministries we stayed full-time, but Carol came home once a month to Russellville to get our mail, pay the bills and see that the house was in good shape. This meant a great deal of driving for her, which she did quite well.

Early in 1990 the First Christian Church at Bowling Green, Kentucky, asked me if I would come for an interim ministry when their pastor retired. I agreed to come by September, but in the meantime the First Christian Church at Greenville, Kentucky asked me to serve them. I accepted with the understanding that I would have to leave for Bowling Green in the fall. Greenville was near Russellville so we stayed at home and I drove every day to my new interim. This was interesting, for Dad had served the Greenville church years before and I had spent some time there with him on weekends. The congregation was small but well organized. I did much calling and was active in the community. The strongest supporters I had in the church were two senior elders, one of whom was our old friend, Dr. Gaithel Simpson. He helped me in rewarding the members of my Pastor's Stay-to-church Club. Carol was quite popular, speaking for several occasions.

In June I had a heart attack and was flown by helicopter to Nashville where Dr. William Frist performed four-bypass surgery Dr. Frist later was elected to the United States Senate and served as majority leader of the Senate. It took me some time to recover, but after thirty days I was on my way to Europe, hosting a group of 39. Carol took charge of the tour along with Don and Lillian Nunnelly. We toured Germany, Austria, Italy, Switzerland and France with the highlight being the Oberammergau Passion Play. Carol Lee joined us. I made the trip with no difficulties though somewhat weary. After recovering from surgery I completed my interim at Greenville after six and a half months. But now it was time to go to Bowling Green where Reid Carter had just retired. We arrived just at they started remodeling the office complex and building a new fellowship hall. We were soon very much involved in the life of this dynamic congregation where we would spend a year and a half. Our family had rallied at the time of my surgery and they all came home for Christmas.

Our year in Bowling Green was extremely busy. We finished a fine new office complex and began to use it in a few months. Work on the fellowship hall was slow, but before we left, Carter Hall had been completed and dedicated. It has been widely used by the community as well as by the congregation. We became very much involved in community life, enjoying many basketball games at Western Kentucky University. We lived in the parsonage which was quite large and comfortable with a big yard. We were so close to the stadium that we could listen to the loudspeaker from the football games from our doorstep. For a short time we had Connie's dogs Kegger and Trojan with us and Carol had a bad fall walking them. We found many new friends who gave us great support, including Meredith and Harriet Johnson and Nolan and Ann Fields. We were close enough to Russellville that Carol was able to serve there as president of the Aftermath study club, and she was elected to the State Board of P.E.O., the philanthropic educational organization that would be a major part of her life for years to come. Our home congregation in Russellville celebrated its 150th anniversary and I helped by writing the last fifty years as my Dad had done for the first hundred years. During the year we had a vacation at Disneyworld, spent a week at the Chatauqua Institute in New York, visited with all of our girls and attended the General Assembly of the Christian Church in Tulsa. We lost two beloved pets this year. Carol Lee's Benson died after a struggle with cancer. She took him everywhere for treatment and finally surgery that failed to save him. Carol went to be with her for the surgery and flew his body back home to be buried in the back yard at Russellville. Connie's big dog Trojan was hit by a truck while she was away from home. I met her when she brought him to Russellville to be buried also in our growing pet cemetery. Cathie and Peter were hiking, biking and camping while teaching in Oneonta. Carol Lee was elected President of CHELA in San Francisco, and Connie was playing in two productions of the community theater in McMinnville while serving as industrial relations manager for Bridgestone Tires. We ended a most enjoyable year and a half in our interim ministry at Bowling Green

We began 1992 by moving to Paducah, Kentucky to begin our fifth interim ministry with the First Christian Church there. In May we went to Vanderbilt for the fiftieth anniversary of my graduation, which meant that I became a "Quinq". The next month Carol and I went to Black Mountain, North Carolina for a reunion of those of us who had lived together at the Disciples House during my seminary days. This would become an annual affair for many years. In July we led a group of twenty-one on a sixteen day journey through Ireland, Wales, Scotland and England; Connie enjoyed the trip with us. After a visit with Carol Lee in San Francisco where she was now President of CHELA, we attended the Regional Assembly of the Christian Church in Louisville In October we rushed to Oneonta, New York to greet our new granddaughter, Stefanie Carol Paluch, born the 20th, named for her two grandmothers. She was a beautiful child. Cathie had to take some time off from her family and group counseling, while Peter had assumed some new duties with Hartwick College. Connie with her dog Kegger continued to work with Bridgestone Tires in McMinnville, Tennessee. We came home from Paducah to celebrate Christmas with all of our family in Russellville.

The next year, 1993, began quietly in Paducah, but in March disaster struck. Carol had what should have been routine rotator cuff surgery at Vanderbilt Hospital. However, the anesthetist made a mistake that gave her an infection that made her critically ill. A day after returning home seemingly well she had to be rushed back to the hospital where she was in desperate condition for three weeks, and she convalesced for nine months before getting back her strength. She was able to get to Louisville in the summer for the State Convention of P.E.O.

where she was installed as State Organizer. She had made rapid progress when the whole family gathered to celebrate the wedding of Connie and Ed Hitchcock at the home of Ed's parents, Allen and Bonnie Hitchcock in McMinnville. Carol and I attended the General Assembly of the Christian Church in St. Louis before we returned to Paducah for a very satisfying farewell as we closed our ministry there after a year and a half. In August we were able to visit our granddaughter, Stefanie Carol Paluch in Oneonta, New York with a week in New England before celebrating Carol Lee's birthday in the Napa Valley. Carol's P.E.O. duties took her to Des Moines, Atlanta and across Kentucky in the next three months. But we had had time this year after Carol's illness to enjoy our side porch in Russellville. We were all home for Christmas just after we began another interim ministry with the First Christian Church in Chattanooga, Tennessee.

In spite of some health difficulties 1994 was a good year. We had a successful interim ministry in Chattanooga, ending in May, thinking that this would be our last interim. Connie and Ed bought a new home in Tullahoma, Tennessee which they enjoyed with Connie's dog Kegger. It was halfway between their places of work, Ed still with Bridgestone Tires in McMinnville and Connie now Human Resources Manager for Jack Daniels Distillery in Lynchburg, Tennessee. About the same time Carol Lee bought a home in Mill Valley, California while continuing as CEO for CHELA in San Francisco. She had a new pup, Mattie. Cathie and Peter were kept busy by a precocious two-year-old, Stefanie. Peter was still at Hartwick College and Cathie continued her practice in mental health at Oneonta. Carol and I drove to California to help Carol Lee move and stayed for a housewarming party on her birthday. Likewise, we helped Connie and Ed move to Tullahoma, and we spent three weeks in Oneonta in the fall. In June we went to Columbia, Missouri where we celebrated our 45th wedding anniversary and later to enjoy Carol's fiftieth anniversary of graduation from Hickman High School. Carol was increasingly active as Second Vice-President of the Kentucky Chapter of P.E.O. In October we celebrated the Fiftieth Anniversary of my ordination to the ministry, with our church in Russellville taking the lead. And the girls established an Endowment Fund in the West Area of the Christian Church in Kentucky in my honor. We were all home again for Christmas.

Contrary to our expectations 1995 was a very busy year: the Disciples Clergy Conference at Lake Cumberland, a ski trip to Vermont with the Paluchs then in Tullahoma and back to see Connie play the "Matchmaker" in the Community Playhouse production of "Fiddler on the Roof", to Carol's State P.E.O. Contention at Jenny Wiley State Park, the reunion of Vanderbilt Disciple House students at Gatlinburg. In June we all went to San Francisco for several days at Carol Lee's Mill Valley home with Mattie while Peter and Cathie ran the Dipsea race up Mount Tamalpais. Then we spent a week as Chaplain at Piney Campground in the Land Between the Lakes. In September Carol had knee surgery and Connie followed suit a few weeks later. We were in Pittsburgh for the General Assembly of the Christian Church and then spent a weekend in Stockbridge, Massachusetts at the Red Lion Inn with Stefie, Cathie and Peter. By this time we had agreed to yet another interim ministry at Guthrie, Kentucky, only twenty miles from home where Dad had been their pastor many years before.

We started serving the First Christian Church in Guthrie, thinking it was to be an interim. But we soon discovered that they expected me to be their regular pastor. As a result we spent two and a half years in this last so-called interim pastorate. Guthrie was a congregation of older families with very few young people, but those families were very faithful. Consequently we had thirty or more in church every Sunday. I had a nice office off the fellowship hall, with a very attractive sanctuary. We had an organist, the only other staff member. They had no secretary but the office was well equipped with provision for producing the Sunday bulletin, which I did every week. I lived at home but drove the twenty miles to Guthrie five days a week and Carol came with me on Sundays. I spent most mornings in the office and called every afternoon. With the small congregation I was able to visit every family many times while I was there. I called on prospective members, but there were few possibilities and I had little success in attracting new members. But the congregation was very active with a good women's group and monthly church dinners. There were several fine families who gave good leadership to the church—Dean and Jeane Moore, John and Jeri Allensworth, Helen Davis, Coleen Dorris, Robert and Jean Downer, John and Elizabeth Jennings, Robert and Susan Menees among others. I had few weddings or funerals while I was there but the year after I left, seven of the older members died, leaving the congregation still smaller. During this time Carol was active at home, helping with Historic Russellville, Habitat for Humanity, and giving strong support to her P.E.O. chapter. During the first year at Guthrie Carol and I were able to visit our families and have us all home for Christmas.

I continued serving the Guthrie church during all of 1996. I was in the office five days a week, called on all the members and prospects, attended Board meetings and family night dinner, participated in the Ministerial Association, had one funeral and two weddings. Carol and I saw many doctors through the year. In February we left for a cruise through the Panama Canal, which we had already planned. We left from Los Angeles and landed in Florida. In April we went to Chattanooga for a P.E.O. Convention, then back to Tullahoma where we heard Connie's children's choir perform beautifully. The Kentucky P.E.O. Convention came next in Lexington. In May Carol had surgery at St. Thomas. On June 5th we celebrated our 47th wedding anniversary with a dinner in Bowling Green. Carol was in Des Moines in July for P.E.O. We attended the Regional Assembly of the Christian Church in Lexington, then drove to Oneonta for a good visit with the Paluch clan. In September we went to Tullahoma before several days in Memphis. Then Carol entertained her P.E.O. Board at our home. We flew to San Francisco to spend some time with Carol Lee and Mattie in Mill Valley and St. Helena. Later Connie and Ed went with us to Kirksville. During the last of the month Carol had been seeing Dr. Christie, who would take her to surgery early the next January. But in the meantime we were all home again for Christmas.

The Interim Years

In February of 1997 I had double knee replacement. After brief rehab we had to rush to Oneonta for the birth of our grandson, Peter Jacob Paluch, on March 6th. In April we went to Huntsville, Alabama where I participated in the funeral service for my long-time friend Elmore "Scoop" Hudgins. In May we were all in Lexington, Kentucky where Carol was Presiding as State President of Kentucky P.E.O., the culmination of seven years of working up through the preceding offices. She did a masterful job with the assistance of Cathie and Carol Lee who had been initiated in P.E.O. Connie sang in the choir but she was not initiated into P.E.O. until November. I took care of Petie, who was only two months old. The next month we all gathered at Camden, Maine for a week on the east coast plus some time in Boston with a Boston Pops concert and a visit to Old North Church. Then we went to Seattle for the International Convention of P.E.O. where Carol was a delegate. While there we spent two days at Vashon Island with Polly Coffman, going with her to Victoria and Vancouver. We had two visits in Oneonto and a vacation with Carol Lee and Mattie in Mill Valley. Connie and Ed took us to the Opryland Hotel where we had birthday dinner at Bouregard's for Carol Lee's birthday. We had a sad time when Connie's dog Kegger died at sixteen. Connie and Ed still had a rambunctious young Dalmation named Pepper. After a busy year with surgery and illness we were all glad to be home for Christmas in Russellville.

Although we started 1998 in the normal way with Vanderbilt basketball games, it became obvious that Carol was having difficulty walking. We went to the Mayo Clinic in Jacksonville, Florida where we stayed with our friends Jim and Dudley Seale while seeing the doctors, who confirmed the fact that she was suffering from allergies but would soon need knee surgery. So in September she had both knees replaced by Dr. Christie who had done mine two years earlier. After ten days in rehab at Vanderbilt she was soon walking better than was I. We had good visits in Oneonta for birthdays, Peter Jacob's first in March and Stefanie's in October, with Connie and Ed and their dogs Pepper and Frank in Tullahoma, and with Carol Lee and Mattie in Mill Valley. We went to Missouri twice that summer: for the fiftieth anniversary of Betty Jo and Bob Dunkeson in Jefferson City and Betty Ann and Dale Powell in St. Joseph. We went to see Uncle Robert and Aunt Helen Powell in Columbia and Sue and Chris Christiansen in Huntsville, Alabama. Then to Black Mountain, North Carolina for the annual reunion of Disciples House alumni at Christmount, to the Kentucky Regional Assembly in Frankfort and the Retired Ministers and Spouses at General Butler State Park in Kentucky, and to Louisville for Carol's state P.E.O. Convention. When at home Carol and I were busy serving as elders in our church, and with Habitat for Humanity and Historic Russellville which was restoring the historic Saddle Factory. I supplied a few Sundays at nearby churches and had an occasional funeral. And always we had good visits with all of our families. I had four surgical procedures during the year—for hydrocephalus, cataracts twice and trouble with my foot, but none was as difficult as Carol's. Needless to say, we were happy that the entire family would be home in Russellville for Christmas.

On June 5, 1999 Carol and I celebrated our fiftieth wedding anniversary with a dinner and evening in which the girls recalled the main events of those fifty years with music, narrative and slides. Stefanie danced, we had many pictures on the walls, and a wedding cake like the one from our first wedding. Then we left for a cruise on the QE2 for a week in London where we saw 'The Prisoner on Second Avenue" and "Beauty and the Beast". We flew home on the Fourth of July to meet Cathie and Stefanie for a few days in New York City. We went to Oneonta for Stefie's seventh birthday. We spent many weekends in Tullahoma with Connie and Ed, who now worked as an electrical engineer with Sverdrup and Connie began commuting to Chattanooga where she is a professor at the State Community and Technical College. We had our annual reunion of the Disciples House alumni at Vanderbilt, this time at Pigeon Forge, Tennessee, as well as the State P.E. O. Contention in Owensboro, and the 150th anniversary of the General Assembly of the Christian Church. We went to Paducah and Madisonville for anniversary celebrations of the churches we had served, and we went to Huntsville where our friends Chris and Sue Christianson had a reception for us in their home. At home we were elders in our church, served on the Board of Historic Russellville, I served as an election judge and Carol performed jury duty. We enjoyed an anniversary luncheon of my high school class of '38, and worked out regularly at the Carpenter Center. In spite of Carol's asthma and arthritis problems and a prostate procedure for me we stayed free of any surgery until I broke my arm in a fall "on the sidewalks of New York" when we were all there for Macy's Thanksgiving Day Parade. But we still enjoyed the parade, FAO Swartz, "Annie Get Your Gun" with Bernadette Peters and the Rocketts at Radio City Music Hall's Christmas Spectacular. Then for the fiftieth time, Carol and I celebrated Christmas together, along with our family.

We were constantly "on the road again" in 2000: Oneonta for Stefie's dance recital and Petie's birthday, driving home through the Pennsylvania Dutch country, flying to San Francisco where Carol Lee is President of Chela Financial, with her dog Mattie and an Easter dinner on a cruise around the San Francisco harbor and the annual Easter Jazz Festival at Grace Cathedral. Carol Lee had bought her Honda company car and we drove it home, spending two nights in Las Vegas, Yosemite National Park, Grand Canyon, Sedona, Arizona, and visits with family and friends in Kansas and Missouri. Then a weekend in the Hudson River Valley with Cathie and the kids, and home through Philadelphia and Strasburg, Pennsylvania before five days in Washington with Carol Lee who was there for a conference. Home through Richmond to visit my roommate from seminary, Carnie and Margaret Burcham. There were visits with Connie and Ed and their dogs Pepper and Frank in Tullahoma. Connie was in a bad wreck which took her nearly two months to recover. She was still driving five days a week to Chattanooga State Community College and Ed's job with Sverdrup often took him on trouble shooting missions, one of which was in London where Connie joined him for a week. At home we were still busy as elders in our church, Historic Russellville and Habitat. Carol served as President of her local chapter of P.E.O. again. We attended the Regional

Assembly of the Christian Church in Kentucky at Bowling Green, the state P.E.O. Convention also in Bowling Green, Russellville High School class of 1938 luncheon and the Disciples House reunion at Pigeon Forge. We were all home for the Fourth of July when Steffie and Petie rode in the parade.

In March of 2001 we were in Oneonta for Petie's fourth birthday when we received word of the death of Uncle Robert Powell. So we rushed in a major snowstorm to fly to Columbia where I had the service and Connie flew in to sing. We hurried back to Tullahoma where Connie had surgery and then to Florida for a week with Glenn and Dolores Geiger in their condo at Pensacola Beach. On the way home we visited our friends Sue and Chris Christiansen in Huntsville before leaving for Easter with Carol Lee. In May we went to Hot Springs, Arkansas for the reunion of the Disciples House group from Vanderbilt. Then to Louisville for the fiftieth wedding anniversary of Henry and Margaret Campbell. Next we spent a week with Connie and Ed in the Louisiana plantation country, New Orleans and Dauphin Island, Alabama. Carol Lee called to tell us that her beloved dog Mattie had died of a heart attack, so we flew to Mill Valley for the funeral, which I conducted in Bo's yard where Mattie was buried.

In July we were back in Columbia again on the way to the General Assembly of the Christian Church in Kansas City. Then we attended the 200th anniversary of the Cane Ridge Revival in Bourbon County, Kentucky and in August we spent a week with Cathie, Stefie and Petie at Hungry Mother State Park in Virginia. Shortly after the terror disaster of September 11th Carol and I flew to Spain for two weeks at Torremolinos on the Costa del Sol of the Mediterranean, including a trip to Cassablanca in Morrocco. Next we helped Connie and Ed move to a new home in McMinnville, Tennessee with Frank and Pepper. Back to Columbia in November for the fiftieth wedding anniversary of Glenn and Dolores Geiger before spending Thanksgiving with Carol Lee where the Paluchs joined us to celebrate Cathie's fiftieth birthday and Carol's seventy-fifth. But we still found time to serve as elders in our church and work with Historic Russellville and Land of Logan Habitat for Humanity in building three new homes. Carol completed another year as President of Chapter AB of P.E.O. and I got to play once more with the Vanderbilt Alumni Band at the Homecoming game. By that time we were ready to be home for Christmas.

2002 started quietly. We saw "South Pacific" in Nashville. In April we flew to Oneonta for a visit to Cooperstown and Mystic, Connecticut. Then we drove to Pensacola for a week with the Geigers in their condo. Then several days with family in Columbia. In May I attended a Kiwanis Lt.Governor's Conference at the Cumberland Inn in Williamsburg, Kentucky. From there we went to Gatlinburg for the Vanderbilt alumni reunion. Next came Carol's P.E.O. convention in Louisville. We went to New Orleans for the Kiwanis International Convention. We spent a day in July at Beech Bend Park with all our family, including Bradley. In August we attended the Kiwanis District Convention in Franklin, Tennessee. Then we went to Columbia for a CSC reunion. I spent a good bit of time in Guthrie organizing a new Kiwanis Club Then the Kentucky Regional Assembly in Middletown, Kentucky. I was very busy all fall attending to my duties as Lt. Governor. I arranged for the visit of our Kiwanis Governor to our division with a dinner at our club in Russellville. We drove to Oneonta for Stefanie's birthday.

All this year there had been a growing movement to separate our congregation from the Disciples of Christ by an independent movement. For this reason I invited our regional minister, Jan Ehrmentraut, to preach for us and meet with the elders. She did a good job, but the elders were not very kind to her. We celebrated Carol's birthday and went back to McMinnville for Thanksgiving and Connie's birthday. In December we enjoyed a Christmas time cruise on the Danube River with Connie, Ed, and Carol Lee. We were happy to have us all home for Christmas.

Much of the year 2003 involved my service as Lt. Governor of Kiwanis. This meant three visits in the year to all twelve clubs in the Division, from Glasgow, Kentucky to Dover, Tennessee plus installations and special events. I served with Asa Bishop, Governor of the Kentucky-Tennessee District, attending the Mid-Winter Conference in Chattanooga, two International Conventions in Indianapolis and the Kentucky-Tennessee Convention in Owensboro, Kentucky. We had good visits with the Paluch family, Connie and Ed, and Carol Lee with her new dog Charlie. Then a few days in Essex, New Hampshire, a week again with the Geigers in Pensacola, the annual reunion of the Disciples House group back at Christmount in Black Mountain, North Carolina, a few days at the quaint village of Rugby in Tennessee, Louisville for the wedding of our niece Jennifer Coffman to Jacob Ragland, a week with the family on the Outer Banks of North Carolina, and the General Assembly of the Christian Church in Charlotte, North Carolina. We attended the 75th anniversary of the Disciples House in Nashville. Carol and I were involved in our usual activities and I helped Russellville High School start its first reunion. Of course we all made it home for Christmas.

In 2004 I was spending a good deal of time preparing to publish The Story of Logan County. We spent a lot of time with Paula Cunningham, the manager of the Clanahan Publishing Company that would produce it. With the help of the girls we made decisions about style, cover, number of copies, price, methods of promotion, etc. It would not be ready until summer, but in the next few months we would be constantly on the go. Early in March Carol and I went to Oneonta for Petie's birthday and soccer. After a brief visit to McMinnville we returned to Oneonta for a good visit, including some time in New England visiting Plymouth and Cape Cod. Then to Columbia where Carol Lee was being honored as a distinguished alumna by Columbia College. We enjoyed the tribute they paid her and sat in on two of the classes to which she spoke. We left immediately for North Carolina to the reunion of the Vanderbilt Disciples House group at Christmount.

We celebrated our 55th wedding anniversary at Mentone Springs, Alabama, a gift from Connie and Ed. I took time out to have a defibrillator installed at St. Thomas Hospital before we flew to San Francisco to visit Carol Lee.

Now the Story of Russellville had come from the publisher and it was time for its introduction and book signing at Historic Russellville on July 15th. It was received with much fanfare and we sold close to nine hundred volumes the first day. We were ready for a vacation, so we left immediately for a week with the family on the Outer Banks of North Carolina to celebrate Carol Lee's fiftieth birthday. In August Carol and I were joined by Parker and Jean Rossman for a cruise down the Danube River through five countries recently freed from Communist domination, to the Black Sea. We returned just in time for the Kentucky-Tennessee Kiwanis Convention in Clarksville, Tennessee. In September we attended the Regional Assembly of the Christian Church in Kentucky at Owensboro. Then we hurried to Tulsa, Oklahoma where I married Carol's cousin Linda Lewis to Mike McWilliams. Coming home we spent some time seeing the shows and a Broadway musical at Branson, Missouri, before visiting Carol's cousin Ailene and John Wood in Preston, and friends in Columbia. We returned to Columbia in October for Carol's reunion at Hickman High School and a visit with the Geigers, By Christmas we were happy to have us all back home together.

As 2005 began Carol was recovering from a broken leg and living on oxygen, but we still were able to make several visits to our children. We flew twice and drove once to Oneonta for Stefanie's dance recital, her sixth grade graduation and her role in "The Nutcracker". Both Stefie and Cathie danced in "Á Night at the Grammys" and Petie was making a name for himself in soccer. Cathie was still busy with her psychiatric counseling and Peter was now teaching at the State University of New York in Delhi, while spending many hours teaching handicapped people to ski. They had a new Chihuahua puppy named Mocha. We also flew to Mill Valley where Carol Lee with her dogs Charlie and Scooter was remodeling her house. She spends some time with trips to New York serving on the board of an insurance company plus volunteer work and other community boards. We made many visits to McMinnville with Connie and Ed and their good dogs, Frank and Pepper. The climax of the year was when we all spent a week in October as their guests in a beach house on the Gulf of Mexico at St. George Island. Carol especially enjoyed the time on the beach. I spent a day selling my book at the Kentucky Book Fair in Bowling Green and stayed busy with Kiwanis, Habitat and the First Christian Church where Carol and I remain as elders. Carol kept our old Coffman home inviting, working in P.E.O. and the Aftermath Club. We met with my RHS class of 1938 for its annual reunion. We were happy to be home in Russellville for Christmas.

Just as we were to resume our normal activities in 2006, Carol's spinal stenosis flared up and her spine began to deteriorate. She was having difficulty standing and walking. But we were able to drive to Cumberland Falls for the reunion of retired ministers and wives before going on to Gatlinburg for several days with Cathie, Stefie and Petie. From there we went to Ashville for a visit at the Biltmore Estate before the annual reunion in North Carolina with our Disciples House graduates. In May I flew to California to drive back with Carol Lee and her dogs to Russellville. Then we both drove with Connie to see Cathie and Stefie in a dance recital in Oneonta. I flew back home to meet my cousin from Jacksonville who wanted to visit our home where her grandmother was born. Carol Lee then took Cathie, Stefie and Petie on a great trip across country through Mount Rushmore, Yellowstone, the Tetons and Lake Tahoe to Mill Valley. By this time Carol's condition had deteriorated so that we had several months of virtual inactivity, but we had weekend support from Connie and Ed. But we were able to get her back to Florida for another week on St. George Island. We also celebrated Carol's 80th birthday with a stay at Paris Landing State Park with Connie, Ed, and Bonnie and Allen, Ed's parents. We lost some good friends during the year—Bob Dunkeson, Don Pittenger, Mildred Shrout, Curt Winn and Mary Rucker. But we were thankful to have us all home for Christmas.

For my 85th birthday in 2007 we had several friends in for dinner. Cathie, Stefanie and Petie came to take us to General Butler State Park for the Retired Ministers Retreat. But then in May I woke up one morning with severe pain in both legs, unable to walk. After two long months of tests it turned out to be a herniated disc, which required surgery, a lumbar laminectomy. Following rehab at SOKY in Bowling Green I was able to walk again, but with a cane. We were able to go to Madisonville for the All-Disciple Sing where I sang with the Russellville choir in the church where I had been the pastor for twenty years but never was asked to sing in their choir. In September Carol fell going into church and broke her hip. Surgery and extensive rehab got her up and going again About this time I had a partial corneal transplant to improve my vision. In October Carol Lee took us to Columbia for the 175th Anniversary celebration of the church where Carol grew up and I had been Associate Minister and Director of Student Work for twelve years. We had a great reunion and spent time with former members of the Christian Student Congregation. Cathie was busy with her psychiatric social work and Peter was teaching again at Hartwick College in addition to his job at SUNY Delhi. Stefie wss busy with dance, music and performance in special programs while Petie at ten was starring in soccer in addition to music and art. Carol Lee at Mill Valley became a golfer, playing weekly in a league while making several trips a year to New York serving on the board of a life insurance company. She also volunteered on the boards of two non-profits in San Francisco. Connie and Ed with dogs Pepper and Frank were living in McMinnville while she commuted to class as professor of business management in Chattanooga State Community College and Ed was an engineer with the Arnold Space Center. Carol was very much involved in church groups and PEO, finally walking much better, while I continued to sing in the church choir and met regularly with Kiwanis and Historic Russellville. We were grateful after such a difficult year to have all of us home for Christmas.

Carol and I were taking care of each other pretty well at home as 2008 began. But she was not very strong and having difficulty eating her meals. The girls talked to us about the possibility of moving to an assisted living situation but Carol resisted strenuously. Finally, she reluctantly agreed to go, but then sobbed sadly at the possibility of leaving our home. We did move the first of March to a very attractive room at the Beehive (BHI), the Baptist home for assisted living located in Russellville. Carol Lee came to help us move and decorated our new room quite attractively. But we had only been there two days when Carol began to have great difficulty swallowing and was taken to Logan Memorial Hospital. When her condition grew rapidly worse Dr. Hayden had her moved to the Medical Center in Bowling Green where she was critically ill. Dr. Arshad. Dr.Arhmed and Dr. Gaba pulled her through one crisis after another when we wondered if we could save her. Carol Lee and I stayed at the Holiday Inn and Connie came regularly. We had good help from Harriet and Meredith Johnson, Ann and Nolan Fields, Bill Adams and Barbara Bush. But Carol finally began to recover enough that we were able to take her to a rehab facility in Bowling Green temporarily. Soon, however, her condition deteriorated again and so back to the hospital. After a time, we were able to move her to McMinnville where she was in NHC, the rehab hospital, for four months. I stayed with Connie and Ed during that time and we had excellent assistance from Bonnie Hitchcock who stayed with us many days. Connie took Carol to the hospital in McMinnville several times, twice for help at St. Thomas Hospital in Nashville and once for treatment by a doctor at Vanderbilt Hospital. Carol was receiving excellent care and making slow progress. But the time came that the hospital told us they had done all they could for her and would have to dismiss her. Carol had desperately longed to go home, so we tried to find care for her in Russellville, but to no avail. Finally, we brought her home and set up a virtual hospital to provide the oxygen, feeding tube, trachea and suctioning equipment that she needed. Carol Lee came home and organized round the clock nursing care. Connie came up regularly, Cathie often, and many people gave us wonderful support. This was not an easy time, but we made life quite pleasant for Carol. She began to enjoy life at home even though without her trachea she could not talk without a valve in her throat. When she got ready for each day she would put on her makeup and earrings and be ready to face the world. She read the newspaper, enjoyed her many friends, fed cheese to Charlie and Scooter, and we played cards nearly every evening. Frail as she was, her mind was clear and strong. She remembered people, dates and events which I had long ago forgotten. We celebrated her birthday on November 13th with a reception when more than fifty of her friends came to greet her. We enjoyed Thanksgiving. And we were able to open our Christmas gifts beneath a live tree in her room. Carol had come home for Christmas.

Life went on fairly well as 2009 began. We celebrated my 87th birthday, Valentines Day and Easter. In June Carol and I invited our friends for a reception celebrating our sixtieth wedding anniversary. Carol greeted the large group, but it was to be her last open house. She continued to grow weaker and one night she drew her last breath in her own bed at home with me and Carol Lee at her side. Her lungs had finally given out after a long hard fight. It was August 23rd, 2009.

After many came to pay their respects at our home, the funeral service was Friday, August the 28th in our Russellville church where Carol was an elder. Patricia Wright played "Going Home" as our pastor Lee Young and Tom Wright led the service with scripture and prayer. The congregation sang Carol's favorite hymn "The Church's One Foundation" and Larry and Karen Blondell sang "Tarry With Me, O My Savior" that had been sung at every Coffman funeral for years. Connie and I both brought memories of Carol's beautiful life before she sang "How Great Thou Art" and our friend Don Nunnelly spoke. Carol was buried in the Coffman lot at Maple Grove Cemetery.

Carol Lee and her dogs Charlie and Scooter had been with us for a year and now it was time for them to go home to Mill Valley. Carol Lee and I drove to her home, spending a week there. Then I flew to Oneonta to spend a week with the Paluch family—Cathie, Peter, Stefie now a junior in High School, Petie in his first year in Middle School, and their dog Mocha. Then I came to Russellville where I am living alone at home with the help of Cocoa who comes five days a week to fix my meals and Diane who cleans the house and the yard. I spent Thanksgiving week with Connie and Ed in McMinnville and their dogs Frank and Pepper. We decorated our home for Christmas just as Carol loved to do so we could all come home for Christmas once more. With the help of Stefanie I sang "O Holy Night" at the Christmas Eve service.

Family Home on Seventh Street

Seventh Street house decorated for Christmas

50th Wedding Anniversary

Front: Ed Coffman, Stefanie Paluch, and Carol Coffman,
Back: Ed and Connie Hitchcock, Cathie, Pete and Peter Paluch, Carol Lee Coffman

With the Grandchildren, Stefanie and Pete; Christmas

Tree in Front Hall, Russellville

Carol's Dickens Village Collection

Margaret Campbell, Cathie Paluch, Edward Coffman, Connie Hitchcock,
Carol Lee Coffman, Bradley Coffman, Carol Coffman, and Henry Campbell

Epitaph

Once our family was satisfied that I could be content to live alone, my life continued to be active again. Bo and I flew to Florida for my birthday. We drove from Tampa to Naples, visiting many friends along the way—Don and Lillian Nunnelly, Stan and Doris Bohon, Vicki Walker and several others. We returned by way of Brooksville and visited Linda and Larry Altbaum, Bo's friends from San Francisco. My Grandmother Coffman had taught school in Brooksville many years ago. In May Connie and I drove to Lexington for the Kentucky P.E.O. Convention where they were honoring Carol in their Time of Remembrance with a beautiful tribute to her service as State President and her great sense of humor. I flew to Mill Valley in June where Bo and I saw "Wicked" and spent a day at the U.S .Open in Pebble Beach before we flew to Florida for a week with all the family at Disneyworld. We had come to see Stefanie competing in a national dance contest. She did quite well, coming home with a trophy. We stayed at the Coronado Springs Hotel in the center of the park. We saw the Harry Potter exhibit and ride, toured the Animal Kingdom, the Magic Kingdom, Hollywood Studios, and the city center. Even with my cane I rode all the rides and enjoyed all the shows, especially "It's a Small, Small World". I had a motorized cart which made it quite easy to see the whole park and even drive up to our room at the hotel. There are some advantages being handicapped, for it helps you to get ahead of the lines. In September I returned to Bo's and we saw the last two games of the San Francisco Giants baseball team when they won the division championship. So it was great fun watching them on TV for the playoffs and winning the World Series. Our family met for Thanksgiving at Tygart Lake State Park in West Virginia. It was half way between New York and Tennessee for all of us except Carol Lee who spent Thanksgiving with friends at Carmel, California.

This has been a time of remembering the sixty wonderful years since Carol and I were married. She pledged her love to me "...for better, for worse, for richer, for poorer, in sickness and in health, till death us do part." She was ever faithful to that commitment, never once questioning our devotion to each other. Carol was the only child of Frank and Lenora Alexander, who gave her devoted support in all that she did. She had the best education, graduating from Hickman High School in Columbia, Christian College, the University of Missouri, and graduate study at Murray State University. She was the consummate pastor's wife, always encouraging me in my ministry and supporting it in amazing ways. She was a devoted mother rearing our three girls with careful guidance and love. At the same time she founded and established an outstanding Nursery School, sponsored youth groups, taught Sunday School classes, planned and spoke for her annual Lenten Lunches, advised the women's fellowship, and promoted many worthwhile projects. As I look back on my life, I wonder how I could have made it without her constant advice and support. Those were sixty Happy Years, full of vitality and enthusiasm. I miss her dearly. I continue to talk to her each day as if she were here with me. And still each night I sing to her as I had done for so long:

> "Smile awhile I sing you sad adieu, While the clouds roll by I'll dream of you,
> Let me hold your hand in mine, Till another day." — Goodnight, sweetheart!

Now I am continuing to live an active life. I sing in our church choir, serve as an elder, call on the homebound, serve on committees in Kiwanis which I attend each Friday. I eat lunch each Sunday with friends from the church. Each year, I attend the Retired Ministers Conferences with the help of my good friends, Bill and Bicky Shiphorst. I continue to make calls at the nursing homes, and mentor several young pastors as they begin their ministries.

I spend time with Cathie, Carol Lee and Connie and their families. I had hoped to make one more cruise, this one to Scandinavia and St. Petersburg, something Carol and I had planned to do before she was too sick to travel. Carol Lee and I were able to accomplish this last summer, and then, this year, we all went on a wonderful cruise to Alaska. And the entire family spent a wonderful week following Christmas this past year at St. George Island.

I am not sure I understand just what heaven is like, but I know Carol is there and hope she knows how we remember her.

> "I know not where His islands lift their fronded palms in air,
> I only know I cannot drift beyond His love and care."

As I come to the conclusion of *Happy Years ... And Many More,* I reflect upon my ministry and what has been my theme song, Washington Gladden's meaningful hymn:

> "O Master, let me walk with thee in lowly paths of service free;
> tell me thy secret; help me bear the strain of toil, the fret of care.
> Help me the slow of heart to move by some clear winning word of love;
> teach me the wayward feet to stay, and guide them in the homeward way.
> Teach me thy patience; still with thee in closer dearer company,
> in work that keeps faith sweet and strong, in trust that triumphs over wrong.
> In hope that sends a shining ray far down the future's broadening way;
> In peace that only thou canst give, with thee, O Master, let me live."

This has been my ministry.

Ed and Carol in Retirement

Connie and Ed Play Pool at St. George Island

At Red River

Celebrating New Educational Building at Madisonville with
Don McLaughlin and Tom Steiner

Celebrating My 90th Birthday

Visiting Alaska with the Girls and the Hitchcocks

Celebrating Ed Hitchcock's 50th Birthday

Rooting for the San Francisco Giants with Carol Lee

Celebrating Cathie's 60th and my 90th in St. George Island

My Loving Wife, Carol Jean Alexander Coffman

www.ingramcontent.com/pod-product-compliance
Lightning Source LLC
LaVergne TN
LVHW061253060426
835507LV00017B/2050